Ten Thousand Flowers

Stories From the New Ming Quong

Nona Mock Wyman

2nd Edition

Updated with Web Links & New Stories

Photograph/Drawing credits:
- book cover photo – *'Nona with Nail Guards'* - photo by Jim Wyman
- Nona's photo by Erica Hatfield
- flower sketch by Ana Valdez
- *'Girl on Branch'* by *'Don't You Want to Peek?'* – permitted by Lisa Wing
- store photo by Bob Joe
- Jerry Ball photo by Susan Tripp Pollard
- Nona with Buddha Face photo by Lani Phillips
- Dragon Lady card by Carol Lutz
- Flowers by Taylor Callan

Note: Nona Wyman and 'Haiku Poets' works may have been previously published in other anthologies, print or on-line publications in their current or slightly different form. All work printed by attributed authors' permission.

Cover design by Donna Van Sant
Interior book design by Donna Van Sant

dvs Publishing
2824 Winthrop Ave.
San Ramon, CA 94583

Ten Thousand Flowers - Stories from the New Ming Quong/ Nona Mock Wyman
October 2016 2nd Edition with Web Links & New Stories

ISBN: 978-0-9908075-9-9

Printed in the United States of America

*Especially for my 'Ming Quong' customers,
whose sharing and interactions have
made my life memorable.*

(And to you, my new reader.)

Acknowledgements

My Heartfelt Gratitude goes to:

My mentor, Jerry Ball.

The Tuesday Night Poetry Group at Barnes and Noble in Walnut Creek, California. For Barnes and Noble, my appreciation for our special 'corner' for six years!

My endorsers—Dick Bolles, Jerry Ball, and Gary Bogue.

Also to all the contributing 'haiku poets;' included are poems from Ming Quong customers, friends, and upcoming poets of Parkmead, plus a Ming Quong Home alumna's two granddaughters.

Special accolades to my 'unique contributors,' each one contributing their time and special talent in making this book and the world more colorful! Lissa, Lexi, Rachel, Linda Donaghue, Vera Zaskevich, Carol Lutz, Ana Valdez, Taylor Callan, Avery Godfrey, Christina Moline, Tom Chan, Donna Van Sant, my Book Shepherd, Jim Wyman, my Ming Quong customers and friends, and for the unexpected teachers along this 'flowered pathway.'

This New 2nd Edition

This revised edition includes 8 new haibun/chapters, a haiga with picture, more haiku and web-links to an interview and a video.

Name Change: 'EMQ Families First' will be changing their name to 'Uplift Family Services.' Our original name, 'Ming Quong' - radiant light - will be remembered forever by us MQ women. From our humble beginnings to the expanded care of today, this institution will continue to radiate. A 150th anniversary celebration is in the planning for 2017, headed by a former Los Gatos mayor.

Note: EMQ = Eastfield Ming Quong. Eastfield was the 1st orphanage in San Jose. It merged with MQ decades after my time.

Contents

Ten Thousand Flowers

Ten thousand flowers. Imagine that! The first scene I envision is a valley of flowers as far as I can see!

My flower saying is reminiscent of an ancient Chinese line I've used for my haiku (poem) that has appeared on my scroll. To me, *ten thousand flowers* also represents beauty, peacefulness and the abundance of life's gifts.

When I look back at my childhood and life – from orphanage-living to becoming a senior, and now operating my Ming Quong store – memories, like a thousand echoes, surface.

These memories are mainly about 'life's flowers' as good experiences. Some flowers are breath-taking, some conjure up smiling faces, others are velvet soft, while some have fragrances that soothe your soul.

Then, unexpectedly, a few spring up full of thistles, yet appealing with its drawbacks.

As in the cycle of flowers and the cycle of life, negative happenings appear like 'weeds,' but when 'pulled' out and 'banished', I've learned that the 'weeds' have also enriched my life, as in 'lessons learned.'

> breathing in deeply
> may we inhale
> life's fragrances

Tuesday Night Poetry

The second Tuesday of each month is poetry night at Barnes and Noble in Walnut Creek, California. An evening anticipated with joy.

It began when Jerry Ball, the renowned poet, introduced himself at my Ming Quong store in 2008. I enjoyed talking to this Zen-like man, with his quiet demeanor. He mentioned about starting a poetry night volunteering his time. I was interested. He left his haiku books to be sold on consignment at the store. While thumbing through his books, I felt a feeling of reverence; a master was in our midst. The past president of The Haiku Society of America, with awards won locally and in Japan. And recently, an honored position as the curator for the America Haiku Archives in Sacramento.

This man also had a wonderful sense of humor. Just talking to him in normal conversations words would quietly burst forth with his uncanny wit and I'd find myself giggling in a quiet lady-like way!

Shortly thereafter, on April 12th, 2008, the Barnes and Noble Tuesdays Poetry evenings became a reality for all under his tutelage. Frequently at poetry nights I would mention an incident in my life and Jerry would always say, "Write about it."

I tried. First, writing my story in haiku, which I found limiting. Second, writing prose which was too extensive after years of writing two books. Then one day I read some haibun from the Pasadena poetry group Jerry had started in 2002 in Southern California, where he taught philosophy at California State University in Long Beach. As Jerry expounded on this Japanese way of writing I felt this was my new venue. Haibun was not too short or too long for expressing my thoughts, life's lessons and experiences.

> haibun introduced
> combining prose with haiku
> and this book came forth...

Also included are some haiku, haiga, tanka and senryu.

The Birth of a Haiku

up the pathway
across the silent valley
ten thousand flowers

"When you read a haiku for the first time and it is accepted by your peers, a haiku is born. That," said Jerry Ball, our haiku teacher, "is the Japanese style." So in 2011 the above haiku was born on a Tuesday night at Barnes and Noble in Walnut Creek, California, but conceived in Indonesia!

From a small intimate group of passionate poets and accolades from our mentor, Jerry, this haiku sailed across the Pacific Ocean to the other end of the world, Indonesia, where, like nature, it flowered and bloomed onto a woven scroll.

INE, an importer and wholesale company of esoteric art works from Indonesia, created this scroll for their line with its unique texture.

first showing ~ Gift Show
international buyers
partook of haiku

This textured scroll is made from the roots of vetiver and is known as the 'fragrant plant.' It is found in Indonesia, where I visited in 1984. I instantly fell in love with the overall beauty of this lush land. Wonderful feeling that my scroll came from my favorite vacation spot, Indonesia!

from different cultures
a textured haiku was born
furthering Oneness

Japanese Poetry Forms

Haibun

Haibun combines prose and haiku. The range of haibun is broad and frequently includes autobiography, diary, essay, prose poem, short story and travel journal.

Haiku

'Traditional haiku' contains 17 syllables divided into 3 lines of 5-7-5. It usually pertains to a season, an element of nature, or a moment of beauty. 'Modern haiku' uses the same format, but with fewer, (unnecessary) words.

My haiku, which I've signed 'nona,' are usually in the 'moment.' The contributing poets encompass all the above.

> the haiku
> each with its
> own rhythm
> ~ nona

Senryu

Senryu is haiku with a sense of humor, human nature or emotion.

Haiga

Haiga is a haibun haiku combined with a picture pertaining to the poem.

Tanka

Traditional tanka is similar to haiku. It has five lines with a thirty-one syllable count and five lines of 5-7-5-7-7.

Modern tanka follows today's 'modern haiku,' sometimes using fewer words to express a thought or moment.

Haibun

Part One

Capturing China's Past

behind the antique
nail guards, depicting
Chinese royalty!

At my Ming Quong store, any 'treasure' found and added to our collection of esoteric gifts can be exciting and fun.

This time, they were ornate finger-nail guards from old China.

Five long pointed silver guards adorned with jewels. These were worn by the elite women to protect their nails.

Intrigued, I immediately put them on and felt like an aristocrat from the High Courts of China! Yet, my hand portrayed a feeling of 'witchy empowerment,' as they resembled mini weapons!

I needed to capture this old part of history, so in a rush between customers, I quickly grabbed a sheer chiffon scarf and draped it across my head. I deftly placed my jeweled hand in front of my face and called out to Jim.

"Hurry," I cried, "Take a picture before someone comes in."

He did, and my faithful, ole-time Polaroid camera slowly inched out a colored photo.

And there I was, a version of a Chinese Empress depicting China's past.

Reflections:

Years later, to my surprise, this 'spur of the moment' picture is now the cover of 'Ten Thousand Flowers' representing

——————————*Royalty* ————————*Mock Royalty!* ——————————

The following haibun/chapter tells the story about my royalty background!

Three Thousand Years Later, My Hawaiian Relatives

Christmas of 2004 was in full swing, when a Chinese man, his wife and sister entered the store near closing. I was tired, but seeing their congenial smiles renewed my energy. They were visiting from Hawaii. We exchanged warm greetings, and talked about their beautiful homeland, when to my surprise I learned their surname was:

> 'Mock,' – just like mine!
> 'the Chinese custom being
> all Mocks are related'

A rare happenstance. I was over-joyed. That's when the man, Dr. Marshall Mock of Kapaa, Kauai, asked if I knew that our village had been renamed.

"Really?" I exclaimed. He relayed how the Emperor had changed our name in honor of heroic deeds performed by our village! Unbelievable.

> flabbergasted
> questions burst forth
> like a waterfall.

They added that our family genealogy contained many historic facts! Before they left the doctor's wife snapped a photo of the new Mocks! What nice relatives! The sister promised they would send me the genealogy.

Four months later, a large envelope arrived with an unfamiliar return address from Oakland, California. I gasped; it was the doctor's sister, Michelle Mock Lindberg, my new-found relative. Inside the envelope, the long-awaited genealogy. Plus an extra bonus, the photo! At that time it was the Chinese Rooster year—my year—so appropriately the rooster called out to me:

> 'wake up — wake up'
> the rooster crowed, 'you've
> got a lot to learn!'

Eagerly I glanced at the numerous pages and facts about my ancestors and China.

> across the sea
> 3,000 years later
> history lessons

The foremost discovery that came across was, we were off-springs of a 'royal family!' Descendants of the second prince of King Sun of the 'Chou Dynasty!'

Our clan was originally from Northern China, but through-out the ages had dispersed to other regions due to China's numerous conflicts. China had been at war and the Mock villagers with their combative strength and endurance fought fiercely resulting in the recovery of the state.

Therefore, in 878 B.C. they were honored by the Emperor.

> knighted Kei to Mock
> the village people
> felt the pride

The above genealogy story began in 1935, when Dr. Herbert M. Kane (Kah-ney) a Chinese optometrist related to the Mock family, made his one and only trip to China as a filial duty to search for the ancestral village.

In a lengthy letter he wrote to his beloved nephew; he stated that in 'The Big Book of Genealogy' the Mock records are displayed prominently in the Ancestral Hall located in the Sun Wah District of the Kwongtung Province. He continued how he immediately had his grandfather's grandson, Mock Lum make a copy of this book, from the beginning of the clan to our branch. And for his family members he had an exact copy of the genealogy made in 1959 by a student from Hong Kong who attended the Stevens Point State Teachers College.

Parts of Dr. Kane's descriptive letter was full of his piety and cultural insights, reminiscent of Confucius. 'Study the language of your forebears and you'll find new doors opening. You'll be richer culturally.'

Learning more about the Mocks, I read the village consisted of 700 souls. Some were diversified, ranging from high officials to a district judge and politicians. However, there was one significant piece of history which embraced me fully. A man named Mock Chai, of the 125th generation, widely educated and a provincial official, had published a collection of poems of his own!

now I know in part
why I am the way I am
my Mock heritage

Reflections:

Throughout the ages many ancestors migrated to Hawaii. This fact reminded me of the on-going question strangers frequently asked me during my life-time, 'are you from Hawaii or are you Hawaiian?'

A wonderful fact discovered, my Ming Quong store customers have always been interested in 'I. Ching.' I, too, have gained more knowledge thanks to them. The I. Ching book, authored by 'Wen Wang,' was one of

the founders of the 'Chou Dynasty!' Confucius, who edited the book,
described it as the greatest of all writings.

Nona (middle) with her Hawaiian Relatives

The True Meaning Of Christmas

It was the winter of 1975, and our Christmas window was decorated with the old-fashioned strings of colored lights.

A manzanita branch hung down the center of the window with handcrafted ornaments representing far-a-way countries. Under the branch was a tiny statue of baby Jesus lying in a manger with his arms reaching upwards, as if waiting to be embraced. Next to the manger was a handmade card with the star of Bethlehem beaming its brilliant rays to the words,

"Happy Birthday Jesus."

The following day a storm blew in to Walnut Creek, and the town was drenched with a torrential downpour. No one was walking the streets. But suddenly, a tall imposing woman barged in. She was dressed completely in black as bleak as the weather! Dripping like a faucet from the top of her pointed rain hat, down to her stylish galoshes. She plopped her umbrella on the floor and I glimpsed a perturbed expression.

woman annoyed
at me, the weather or what?
no, the window!

Our Christmas window? But why? Turned out she was a Christmas judge for the merchant's windows and her annoyance festered from the fact that we did not submit an entry for the contest.

She expounded with no uncertainty that...

window portrayed
the true meaning of Christmas
we would have won!

She left in a huff, with biting words of advice, "Next year submit your name!"

> we listened, we learned
> submitting our name in time with
> Jesus in the manger

And we won! And ironically the woman in black was not even the judge that year. But it made no difference as she was correct, the true meaning of Christmas was every year!

> the first woman
> judging our window:
> Margaret Lesher!

Reflections:

After our encounter Margaret and I corresponded. I thanked her for speaking out and taking the time to truly be a judge and going beyond her job of venting her feelings and reprimanding us! Because it was all done with love! She was the leading society woman of Contra Costa, beautiful inside and out, and a giver of her time for all. When she married Dean Lesher, the newspaper magnet, they were the philanthropists of the county. The Dean Lesher Regional Center for the Arts is a good representative of their endeavors.

One Regret: On Margaret's correspondence she used a red Chinese chop below her name. The chop was a phonetic sound of her name, with no significant meaning. So she wanted me to give her a Chinese name. Honored indeed, my mind buzzed for the longest time; after many thoughts, I came up with the name, "Beautiful Soul." But due to my choosing the perfect name, time had elapsed, and it never came to fruition.

'Beautiful Soul'
always been in my mind
now reborn!

A Lesson Learned: less regrets if faced with a challenging project before you, breathe in deeply, calm your mind, meditate and truly listen to your inner voice and proceed at once!

The second judge was Paula Schiff, a Ming Quong customer. Her husband, Albert Schiff, was a City Councilman.

Then in 1977, a tragedy shocked the community; Margaret mysteriously drowned in a lake.

dark as the night
husband unable to shed
a light...

I attended the memorial services with Robert Ehrhart. Robert was the president of the Camellia Society.
Later his tribute to Margaret; a camellia named for her.

each season – blooming
forever
remembered...

A 'Thank You' to Dr. Al Loosli, (who is my knee doctor) for the above story. During a conversation Margaret's name was mentioned and that jogged my memory of yester-years! Truly a divine interaction!
Dr. Loosli's office on Main Street is next door to the new antique store owned by one of the Leshers.

Stores Dress Up For Christmas

Walnut Creek's Best Win Display Awards

WALNUT CREEK — It was merchant against merchant, display against display.

The winners of the Second Annual Walnut Creek Window Decorating Contest were announced this week. The event was sponsored by the Chamber of Commerce.

In Category A, displays of up to 15 square feet, the first place winner, that took Radio Station KDFM's perpetual trophy, was Ming Quong, 1517 N. Main St.;

Mike Pingatore of the Chamber of Commerce presents Jim and Nona Wyman the KDFM trophy for the display at Ming Quong's.

second place, Courtway's Green Auto Parts, 2031 N. Main St.; third place, Olympic Decors, 1548 Olympic Blvd.

Category B, displays from 16 to 30 square feet, winners were: first place, Rossmoor News perpetual trophy, Home Federal Savings, 1928 Tice Valley Blvd.; second place, Walnut Creek Saddlery, 1548 Locust St; third place, Studio Print, 1323 Locust St.

Category C, displays from 31 to 60 square feet, winners were: Bay View Federal, 1332 N. Main St, the first - place winner also captured the KWUN Radio trophy; second place, Wilson's Bath Decor, 1164 Broadway; third place, Carole's, 1966 Tice Valley Blvd.

Category D, entries from 61 to 100 square feet, winners were: first place, Contra Costa Times trophy, Walnut Creek Chevron, 1805 Ygnacio Valley Road; and second place, The Artifactrie, 1329 N. Main St.

Category E, displays of more than 100 square feet, winners were: first place, the president's trophy, Grandma's Antiques, 2323 Boulevard Circle; second, California Street Nursery, 31 Braodway Lane; third, I. Magnin's, 1301 Broadway Plaza.

Category F, two - dimensional window displays, first place, mayor's trophy, Steffi's 1333 N. Main St.; second, Universal Beauty Academy, 2940 N. Main St.; third, Copper Skillet, 1548 Bonanza St.

1st Place Ming Quong's Window Display

A Stranger Named John Nejedly

he braved the unknown
and found a gem — Walnut Creek's
first coffeehouse!

One Spring morning in 1976, I was at the store/coffeehouse called 'The Melting Pot,' before the name was changed to 'Ming Quong.' All alone, and wishing I was at home tending my garden, the front door opened and in walked a distinguished-looking man, who looked familiar.

Well, I thought to myself, maybe my day may be made brighter.

I greeted him and asked, "How can I help you?"

"I'd like a good cup of coffee, please."

I poured Joe's, (my husband's) thick brew of a very dark coffee into a special Japanese 'double-cup' teacup. This was not the usual coffee mug found in a coffee house. This cup-within-a-cup was ornamental, artistic and it kept one's fingers cool. Definitely Joe's choice, a luxury artistic ware for his small establishment.

I sat down across from this gentleman and gradually the man's familiar face became apparent. It was none other than John Nejedly, our State Senator from our seventh district. I was pleased; imagine an adventurous citizen who dared brave the unknown to try out this new Berkeley-type coffeehouse right on Main street.

That's why he was the man he was; a grand senator! He enjoyed the hearty coffee and was intrigued by its rich espresso. Joe's passion for good coffee often lead to other unique sprinklings, for example a pinch of salt!

Meanwhile I was mesmerized by the Senator's story of how he was the official coffee-maker for his son's summer camp, because he simply made the best coffee. A king-size vat was used for his special brew. What was in this coffee? His secret: a raw egg! Both of these men unique coffee-makers.

After he left, I reflected on our pleasant conversation and realized he may have felt slightly let-down as I'm sure he wanted to meet Joe, a controversial type of guy from Berkeley and now settled in the suburbs!

Joe with his unique coffee house had created a haven for 'thinkers and local musicians' who now had a place to communicate. This was quite different from 'cruising the main.'

Back then, Nejedly never conveyed that message.

> he was after all
> a human engaged
> in his surroundings
>
> unforgettable
> a man of worth
> Margaret's ex-boyfriend!

Reflections:

Years later while writing this haibun, I emailed John Nejedly's daughter, Mary Nejedly Piepho, who was the Honorable Supervisor for the Contra Costa Board of Supervisors. I talked about her father and how I remembered with fondness my 'coffee-time' with him.

Later she bought her adorable, well-mannered daughter, Mariah to the store and I had the privileged of meeting her.

Both of them, a tribute to the saga of the Nejedly family!

In the haibun/chapter, 'The True Meaning of Christmas' John Nejedly's former girlfriend was Margaret Lesher.

Extra – Ordinary, Everyday Lessons

did I hear right?
unexpected sayings
are surprise teachers

Early on the book reading circuit, I had the challenge of reading to a class of third graders at Parkmead Elementary. I was challenged because of their age. My thought was, would the 'orphan' subject pique their interest. Also, I was apprehensive as I had only spoken to adults.

Happily, all went well. After I left, their assignment was to write me a 'thank-you' letter. Two examples:

Dear Ms. Wyman,
    I'm sorry your Mommy
    left you at the orphanage
    but look on the bright side
    at least that's the best story I've ever heard.
                        ~ letter from a girl

And this letter from a boy:

Dear Ms. Wyman,
    Thank you for coming
    and 'waist-ing' your good time.

Once my neighbor Richard Nelson Bolles, a renowned author, had a suite of offices right above my store. He was scheduled for a reading of his book, 'What Color is your Parachute.' I looked forward to attending this reading so I could learn more about presentation.

But I was mainly excited because I knew him! That day at the store I was with a last-minute customer and the minutes were ticking away, but finally the transaction was completed.

I dashed over to the Bonanza Book Store on Locust Street. Plopped myself down in the front seat saved for me by Joy Delara, one of Dick Bolles 'employees.'

I was just in time for his introduction. One of Dick's first words to the audience was:

> "thank you for taking time
> from your busy schedule to
> be here tonight…"

I heaved a sigh of relief, and thought how nice. That relaxed me. I felt like he was talking just to me. I never forgot his welcoming words. It was a meaningful reading. That evening I absorbed every little detail. I watched his inter-action with the audience. I marveled at his calmness, his awareness. It was awesome watching a 'best-selling author' and a 'man-of-the-cloth' promoting his book.

Years later, whenever I have a book reading, I always incorporate Dick's appreciative
> "Thank you…"

And of course included are both the third-grade letters. The line, 'waist-ing your good time' brings instant laughter.

Then, on another different learning experience, I once overheard a conversation with two enthusiastic customers at my store about how they thoroughly enjoyed watching the news on television. They went on and on about the news. Hmmm, I thought who could be so good to illicit such raves?

So I asked, "What channel were you watching as I watch the news every night?"

"Oh no, it's
Huey Lewis and the News"
"Oh, but what channel?"

Reflections:

Dick and I became friends. Once he asked me, "How many Chopstick Childhood books have you sold?" His comment:

"If you sell 500 books, it's considered a best-seller!"

"Really?" I exclaimed for I had sold over that amount. I had assumed to be considered a 'best-seller' the book sales would be in the millions like his! I smiled within, not fully believing his statement!

Each year he had updated his original book to help people who had been jobless like him. For he was once an Episcopalian priest but had to leave the ministry due to some controversy of which even to this day I'm not sure what it was! It sounded political. All I knew was that he was a 'great neighbor.' So that didn't matter to me.

For me, I only heard about him and his life-changing story from his employee. He was, as I gathered, 'a giant figure' in our midst. At that time I knew he had been interviewed on 'Nightline' by Ted Koppel.

My adventure into the sushi world came by Dick's love for that delicacy. One time at his home he had an array of assorted sushi fit for the Prime Minister of Japan. The display was much too beautiful to eat. But with Dick's encouragement I tried one. Loved it. And the second one was even tastier. Soon a third... and I couldn't stop. Then suddenly I couldn't stop running!

to this day
I do not eat sushi
instant lesson!

But, over four decades later, I'm back! As next door to us is, 'Oyama' a fine Japanese Restaurant. Some customers have shared their sushi with me and once again I'm in love.

I learned my lesson
don't over-indulge
in anything!

When my first book, Chopstick Childhood, was almost completed I had thought to ask Dick to endorse my Chopstick Childhood book, but thought he was too far removed from my story content of being an orphan. But I should have asked him because of his background in the church. Although I remembered thinking if only he had been a Presbyterian minister!

Now today my question is, does that really matter?

We are what we are and if the person is fine, go for it, follow your heart and face up to any doubts and discuss it!

As you can see, Dick endorsed this book. I am ever grateful.

Today, my knowledge of Dick Bolles 'life from the past to the present' is beyond admiration!

An update on Dick: as of 2015, 'What Color is your Parachute' has sold over ten millions copies, has been translated into twenty different languages and is sold in twenty-six different countries!

And that report comes from the New York Times, not – 'Huey Lewis and the News!' – although I think I hear their music in the background!

with his faith – Dick
created blessings of
'ten million flowers'

Born In The USA

In good ole California, Walnut Creek to be exact—hundreds upon hundreds of haiku were born, the 'American way!' thanks to Gary Bogue, a beloved Contra Costa Times columnist. His column was about pets and wild life. Knowledgeable and widely respected, readers paid attention to his responses to their questions for forty years.

A true poet, he always included a short relevant meaningful saying at the beginning of his column or a haiku from Lura Osgood, whom I surmised was a friend of his. Reading his column always brightened my morning. Occasionally Gary composed a haiku and I always marveled at his choice of words.

At that time I was writing haiku in the traditional 5-7-5 format, just like Lura, so I always enjoyed watching her meet the challenge of seventeen syllables. Her little gems were always a delight. But one day in 2003, a dismal haiku appeared in the column:

> the season of sadness
> yellow leaves slide like tears
> down Octobers cheeks

This sad haiku bothered me because the weather had been absolutely gorgeous. It motivated me to send a haiku to Gary. I submitted my happy one to him:

> welcome Autumn's gifts
> brilliant leaves twirling, dancing
> on the pumpkin patch

Gary published it and that began my journey into the

'Land of Haiku.'

During the years over 100 of my haiku appeared in his column. I came to sign each haiku after my name with a 'title' — 'Haikuyun'.

As Jerry Ball, the haiku master explained, the actual interpretation for haiku is three syllables, not two, pronounced as 'ha-i-ku.' The first two characters are Japanese and the last character written in Chinese meant:

a Chinese person — that was me — 'Haikuyun!'

Haiku originated in China, then was popularized in Japan.

> absolute fun
> I enticed poets and friends
> to submit haiku

Many haiku were born! Gary's column was in sixteen other newspapers, like the Oakland Tribune and the San Jose Mercury. These haiku were well-read! We all loved Gary. But alas he retired. Poets and readers felt the loss.

> mornings were dimmed
> yet souls rejoiced
> remembering...

Note: more on Gary Bogue in the next haibun, 'Gary, the Columnist.'

Gary, the Columnist

Gary Bogue and I corresponded frequently, mostly fun things about 'nothing' which meant 'everything.' Just a few words from him and I would burst into laughter. We became 'pen-pals.'

One time I sent in a haiku:

> outside my window
> sunset slowly paints the sky
> backdrop for the oaks

His immediate response, "How did you know? Perfect for tomorrow's column." I couldn't wait for the morning paper. To be tuned in was the ultimate.

Next morning...

His column headlined about a 'turkey and a motorcycle!'

Huh? Didn't make sense. Then I realized he was pulling my leg — he was calling me a 'turkey!'

His reply — "No, more like a motorcycle — like varoom — VAROOM!"

Round and around we went till I conceded, but only because I had to go to work.

In this book are some haiku from my Ming Quong customers, some of which were in Gary's column, and of course, a few of Gary's haiku.

One day, Lura, a kind and gentle soul introduced herself to me at my store and we became, as I termed it: 'two friends in haiku.' In 2008 Gary and I were privileged to be Lura's guests at a special Christmas program to honor her fiftieth year with the Diablo Women's Chorale, based on her engaging haiku. The celebrated conductor, Rollo Dilsworth, collaborated with the group and produced an unforgettable experience titled:

'Haiku into Music.'

Sunday afternoon
three haiku poets
enjoying a 'first...'

Go Nona Go — Go

"Ready to go Nona?"

In my mind I was ready to go to a special restaurant, but plans changed. Jim Joachim, (also known as Jim Ocean) heard I was celebrating my 50th birthday. Joachim was like my best friend at work. He worked next door at the Health Food store in our once small town of Walnut Creek. This store was a 'first' back in the 1960's and was thought of as an oddity. I learned a lot of healthy things from a guy so slim you could hardly see him! I had read about the wonders of wheat grass, so what did Jim do? he juiced this expensive green wheat for me before I could stop him. The taste was too foreign for me, in fact it was bad! But Jim sipped it easily and smacked his lips! What a ham!

He always had me laughing.

Jim was also the founder of the new venue happening in town, the well-attended 'Musician's Coffeehouse' which was held at the Unitarian Church in Walnut Creek.

When he knew about my birthday, he immediately said, "I want to compose a song for your 'half-century' birthday!

·

"Nona's clan," as Joachim called us, was introduced. We swelled with pride and humility. At least I did! That fun night was one day after my birthday, held at Stage Two in Walnut Creek. Jim and his group, the Celtic Elvis, were featured for the 'first acoustic music' put on by the Contra Costa Showcase.

> they sang their hearts out
> with eagerness and wit
> performance awesome

The song: "Go Nona Go — Go" sung to the melody of Johnny Be Good.

way down in the wilds of Walnut Creek
take yourself down there and have a peek
you will find a place that you can't help but stop
the door rings out its bells when you're in the shop
it's that funky little place call Ming Quong

Chorus: Go Nona Go — Go, (repeat three times) ending the chorus with 'Radiant Light.'

whether it's a pillow or a horoscope
she'll meet you with a smile or maybe a joke
and if you have some money and a little time
you'll find that you've gone crazy and spent all your dimes
still although you're broke you feel you've done no wrong
you've come addicted to that place Ming Quong

Chorus:

now that the news is out you see I've let it leak
you can find a place to go in Walnut Creek
not just another gift shop where it's all the same
where all the clerks are androids and the stock is tame
yes now you know where all you pretty girls belong
it's that funky little place they call Ming Quong

Chorus:

'Go Nona Go — Go' was well-received and he had the audience join in on the chorus. We laughed and clapped till my hands said 'stop!'

> I was thrilled, the best
> song for being fifty
> fact is, I'm glowing now!

Jim and the Celtic Elvis

Reflections:

The chorus ends with Radiant Light – as Radiant Light means Ming Quong in Cantonese.

Some years later Jim was affiliated with the dynamic music promoter, Bill Graham. The San Francisco Civic Auditorium was renamed the Bill Graham Auditorium. Jim's last name? 'Ocean' was his stage name.

And, an interesting fact; Jim resembled the famous musician Mick Jagger and had been mistaken for him! He told me — once a girl sidled up to him after one of his gigs and that's how he lost his v--------!

Huh? I quizzed. He just grinned and laughed heartily. He was always kidding me! But I got it!

Many years passed and his younger brother came in; the latest on Jim — married with kids from his wife. They were all living in the woods in a 'round' house that Jim had built along the help of his brother.

miss his presence
laughing, smiling and singing –
– was that Mick Jagger
performing outrageously?
it was my friend, Jim Ocean!

Oops, just added a tanka, instead of a haiku!

I broke the rules for Jim!

Historic Changes:

The Health Food store was situated where the 1515 Restaurant is now located. This restaurant was a first with its out-door dining, complete with a fireplace and a TV.

This scene dazzled N. Main St. under the giant magnolia trees, brightly lit at night. This was the place for singles to mingle. The magnolia trees were planted by the City.

Back then, life was simpler, no city regulations; merchants were just asked their favorite tree and it was planted. The owners were the Health food store.

Divine Interaction

talking to a friend
a divine interaction
lead to this story

48 years in business
memories surface
unexpectedly

The mention of the Dean Lesher Regional Center for the Arts (DLRCA) bought back forgotten memories. How could I forget that day when I did something beneficial for the Center?

That was eons ago, so I forgive myself!

It was fearful to do but yet the challenge turned out to be glorious! It happened when a new customer, Mary Stanley, who was in charge of a fund-raising event for the Center, entered my store. She asked, if they could use my store's fashions for their luncheon.

I was pleased. But when asked if I would model I hesitated!

My reply was, "No," simply because I didn't have the confidence. But faced with this persistent woman whom I admired for her involvement with community affairs, I listened.

She reassured me that I would be fine as they were my unique fashions, and there would be others like me modeling for the first time. She also added that a few professionals models had said 'yes,' plus other fashionable stores like Jean Harris had agreed. And to reassure me there would be expert helpers behind the scenes to assist us.

In other words, a show put on by people who knew what they were doing!

My reply, "Oh good, you don't need me to model!" But she persisted, and as I watched her enthusiasm mount, something stirred within me and I was compelled to say, "Yes!"

She was pleased and more surprisingly so was I!

> what to model
> a Lim's original
> instant goodness

For that particular outfit I was happy that I had the perfect Laurel Burch earrings.

Held at the Temple Isaiah in Lafayette, the place was impressive. Tickets were $150.00. That day the room was filled with many elegant ladies and handsome men. Laurel Burch attended with her beau, Les Williams. Before the luncheon she presented me with a token — an adorable, two inch wooden horse, which spoke to me of her style and her sweetness.

Fueled by their presence, along with my other supportive friends, Lissa and Sally, I felt rather calm and blessed by their presence. They all sat at the front table with an unobstructed view!

I modeled two outfits. The first one was a two-piece, over-sized top in deep purple with an Asian abstract design in burnished gold. I teamed it with the matching pants. It was simple and stunning.

My second selection was a Lim's white embroidered top with a splash of lavish tropical flowers in lavender with green leaves and a sprinkle of silver sequins. This was worn with the same purple pants that hugged my ankles. This outfit was accentuated with my silver flats and the Laurel Burch drop earrings, designed with a petite lavender pinkish flower.

As I approached my friends' table, I remembered what a male model had said to me as we were lining up,

"Smile, it's supposed to be fun!"

Those words rang in my ears and I did something out of the norm, I paused for a few seconds and smiled!

And to my surprise, Laurel beamed!

Then, as if to keep the momentum going, the enthusiastic program chairman announced Laurel's presence and her earrings, which I then deftly touched, which was showcased perfectly by my asymmetrical hairdo! In fact, everything was perfect and all the people involved were pleased.

> floating happily
> on Cloud 9
> smiles everywhere...

Reflections:

Courage begets courage! Civic pride enhanced as one becomes a true part of the community.

Simply put, my education in life was enriched.

In the spirit of donation to the Center, the store donated a Lim's original crochet outfit, plus the well-liked London, Paris, Walnut Creek tees as worn by the Walnut Creek Aquanauts at the Olympics. It was exciting watching the biddings, especially as Fred Lacrosse and Terry Lowry were at their finest being the auctioneers.

As mentioned in the beginning haiku, this divine interaction happened because of Dr. Al Loosli, my sports doctor for my knee.

See the haibun/chapter 'The True Meaning of Christmas' for the 'divine interaction.'

To the present: the Lesher Center for the Arts celebrated its Silver Anniversary, twenty-five years ago on October 4, 2015.

Soroptimist — Humanitarianism

what do those words mean
optometrist? a human?
a lesson in words...

Add two more words, 'honorarium' and 'AAUW' to the above words and I've got an English lesson! Not one for the academic scene I opted for what I called, 'freedom from school!' But being who I am, I've asked a lot of questions and learned a lot!

'Honorarium' entered my life as I was to receive one from the AAUW of Saratoga after I read for them from my first book, *Chopstick Childhood*, at the Saratoga Country Club.

Hmm, what did that mean? Joe's sister thought it meant an honorary degree! Found out it meant I would get paid! I couldn't believe it!

Endeavoring to do even better, I prepared doubly well! But I did not prepare myself for what happened that day. Up on stage after greeting over 250 people, I leaned on the podium and it rolled forward! It was scary as I was close to the edge of the stage. I kept my composure and stopped it immediately!

The AAUW (American Association of University Women) never let on that they saw it! Actually there were three authors that day, all local. One was an AAUW woman, her book profiled John Steinbeck; then Joe McNamara former Chief-of-Police for San Jose; his book, *Code 211 Blue*, and me with my *Chopstick Childhood* book. I was the first speaker.

After lunch it was discovered the honorarium was missing! I never received it that day! Joe McNamara, who was now with the Stanford University Hoover Institute's 'think tank,' was running late. He rushed in, sat down at his designated seat and saw an envelope with his name on it and put it in his sports coat. He was unaware that my envelope was under his.

We searched everywhere. Weeks later Joe found the checks!

> my 'playful' thinking
> new book, 'Chief of Police
> absconds with orphan's check!'

Now the word Soroptimist, what did it mean? Did it have something to do with 'optometrist?' Why not? They sound connected, plus they rhymed! I found out they were a group of dedicated women of the Soroptimist International of America from the Alamo-Danville area. They gave many scholarships to qualifying students and awards to meaningful people in the community.

Maureen Little, (a Ming Quong customer) was a member and an instructor at St. Mary's College in Moraga. She had invited me to read there several times to the Women Studies class. It was this Soroptimist group who honored me with the word: 'humanitarianism', a word I couldn't pronounce or even really knew if that word was spelled correctly. The Dictionary and Thesaurus had various spellings with different meanings! But on the evening of the awards I received the impressive framed plaque for 'Woman of Distinction.'

> honored for sharing
> from the heart of a
> grateful woman

This award I dedicate to all the girls and teachers at the Ming Quong Home/orphanage. A copy of this award is on the 'history wall' at the store.

Reflections:

Joe Wyman, my husband studied Criminology in college and revered Joe McNamara and was absolutely delighted to meet him. I found out these two men had something in common. While I read a sensitive chapter in my Chopstick Childhood book, I happened to glance at the two Joes — both their eyes were filled with tears!

A 'fun' memory, the AAUW's photographer wanted a picture of McNamara and I together. We posed, but not to her satisfaction. Her comment, "Come on, you can get closer than that!"

My comment, "But it's the wrong Joe!"

At the book signing Joe McNamara and I both sold all our books!

Many years later, when I heard about Joe McNamara's passing, I went to his website and did something I've never done before. I composed a message of appreciation for him. I wrote of how I was honored to have had a book reading with him... ending with my words of him being a "man with a caring heart." Ready to send the message off there was no 'send' button! Frustrated with nothing else in sight I tried the 'post' button and the letter disappeared! A part of me felt lost, crushed. Darn internet, darn computer! But behold, I found out 'post' meant it was now on the internet! Oh my gosh, for everyone to see! I thought only his family would see it! But this 'error' turned around and became a light! As early on the internet I had read negative letters about his political, controversial career. I felt sad. But interestingly, later, I noticed that with my letter praising him as 'the man with a sensitive heart' that the tone softened. Many 'positive' letters came forth from all walks of life. I felt at peace.

Thank you, Joe!

The 5th Grade Honor

Have you ever been given an 'honor beyond your wildest dreams' from a 'young one?'

No certificate, but straight from the heart of a 5th grader! This rare occasion happened when I was an 'adult!' This was my fourth year volunteering my *Chopstick Childhood* book for 'Read Across America' at Parkmead Elementary School in Walnut Creek. California.

As I entered the classroom, the teacher announced my presence. Immediately excitement was felt as the students rushed around to sit next to their friends. Surveying the room I noticed this lone boy, rather heavy-set, who had not moved, but was sitting alone next to the teacher's desk, which was close to me. About half way through my reading I paused for a second when the boy leaned over and whispered to me:

"This is an honor."

Astonished, I was speechless, such an adult saying coming from a young student! When my reading ended and the students parted, he pushed in his chair and once again repeated:

"This was an honor."

I was completely at a loss for words with such a heartfelt gesture. I could only thank him, but I was able to add, "I appreciate what you've said." He acknowledged me silently.

Eager students surrounded my desk to thank me. Some waited for my autograph. A few students had not realized this part of a reading and dashed back to their desks and came forward with bits of torn paper for my signature.

That was amusing and cute! I felt like a celebrity! These animated children were smiling and so was I, inside and out.

I wondered if my 'new friend' would be in line.

he was not there
yet the youth's presence
enveloped my soul

Reflections:

I felt frustrated, and inept to this soft-spoken, well-mannered boy. I wanted desperately to say something meaningful to convey my gratitude. That day I also felt sad because he seemed like an outcast.

Was he beyond his peers? Was he an old soul?

Or was it only me projecting my feelings?

As people have said, 'volunteers receive more than they give.' Definitely true, for that unforgettable day,

'he was honored'
but indeed — I truly was
'the honored one!'

Dress Well, No Matter What!

When my husband Joe was teaching for the Mount Diablo School District, they had a special event for the teachers and their friends. People were asked to submit a floral centerpiece to be displayed in the auditorium where they would be judged. Joe, being busy with his Educationally Handicapped students, forgot to tell me! I heard about it the night before! Under pressure I sat down to contemplate. I looked around at our small living room in Berkeley and focused in on our corner windows with the six sliding shoji shades which Joe had designed with goza mats. They were trimmed in strips of black wood. Perfect, one of these panels which I loved could work for the backdrop. Next, I scrambled around in our storage cabinet and found extra pieces of goza mats for the base. Relieved, I now concentrated on the theme. It had to be meaningful and peaceful representing the shoji screen's serenity. My eyes fell on a beloved Japanese tea pot a Zen student and his wife had given us for our new home. Small in stature, earth-brown in color with a natural twig for a handle.

> perfect item
> chopsticks were added, resting
> on a small object

Everything harmonized. I was happy; but wondered, would it be enough? Up early the next day but running slightly late, we hurriedly arranged our display in the auditorium's display room. Absorbed in my arrangement we suddenly heard that the program had started. Darting off, we saw that the attendance was good, in fact, it was overwhelming! The audience seemed receptive and eager anticipating the outcome. Towards the end of the program three winners were announced. To my surprise the winners won prizes which I knew nothing about! The third place winner was unknown to me. But the second place winner was a well-known woman named Pember whose lavished arrangement of gold flowers had always placed first in other community activities. When it was time for the first place winner, I looked around the room thinking if Pember wasn't number one, who was? And then the judge's voice rang out: "Nona Wyman!" I gasped! Stunned I walked across the auditorium in a haze all the while thinking to myself:

'I wished I had dressed better!'

After accepting the award, I rushed over to the exhibition room in high spirits to snap a picture. But I was startled by Dan Helix, husband of a teacher, Mary Lou, both of whom I knew. He was sitting in the middle of the room keeping watch over the displays. Dan, a quiet and distinguished man, was, as usual, dressed appropriately in a suit. His emotions were as always in check. I was embarrassed especially by my enthusiasm. He matter-of-factly acknowledged me and pointed to my first place plaque. My high spirits greatly contrasted with Dan's calm demeanor. Later Joe took the picture and off we went to the well-liked McDonalds Nursery, to redeem the prize.

two plants of my choice
swaying
papyrus grass

horsetails
like stalks of bamboo
came home with us

Reflections:

Bill Kwong, the Zen student, and I attended Palo Alto High School. Years later Bill and his wife, Laura, gifted us with the treasured teapot while he was a Zen student in San Francisco. He is now the revered, Jakusho Kwong, Roshi. (Roshi is the title of a Zen master.) He established and founded the Sonoma Zen Mountain Center in 1973, in Sonoma, California. He is affiliated with the Zen Centers in Poland and Iceland.

Dan Helix, the impeccable man who guarded the floral displays became the Mayor for the city of Concord, California, and served on the City Council. He was a decorated retired General in the United States Army and is heralded as a model for veterans.

Looking back, my insignificant dress I wore was actually one of my favorites, easy to grab and put on when you're running late!

I've come to realize, your best is in the moment and what comes from your heart outshines all (in other words, be yourself).

Haiku

Senryu

Tanka

Part One

Haiku

Once I composed a haiku about autumn. I asked Jerry Ball for his comment. His answer surprised me, as it was not about changing a particular word or saying. His thoughtful reply was:

JB – "It's very Zen."

Nona – "What is Zen?"

JB – "Your haiku."

My haiku:

harvest moon
gently focused on the
pumpkin patch

early spring, a friend
brings my favorite fragrance
daphne
> ~ nona
> *for Barbara Young*

one iris blooms
in the middle of winter
the yard is purple
> ~ nona

daylight savings time
after work, complete darkness
I miss my garden
> ~ nona

wisteria bloom
cascading
purple waterfall
> ~ nona

after last night's storm
an Olympic size puddle
five clean, happy birds
> ~ nona

Chinese parasols
hung upside down
blooming lotus
> ~ nona
> *early interior light fixtures at the*
> *Ming Quong store*

"Asilomar" by Carol Lutz

twilight stroll
discovering a new path
I linger

~ nona
*A haiga for Carol Lutz – well-
known local artist*

in the garden
amongst winning camellias
a gnarled oak tree
> ~ nona
> *For Robert Ehrhart's Walnut Creek*
> *garden – Past-President of The*
> *Camellia Society*

at harvest time—my
persimmon man brings bags full
of the season's best
> ~ nona
> *for Ira*

Reflection:

  What a generous friend, Ira. But sadly, due to the drought, the tree produced less this year. In the early days Ira sold his fruit to the 'Good-Nature Store,' the second health food store on N. Main, where the ever-popular Army-Navy Surplus store was. It is now a Brandy Melville clothing store.

God bless you!
and I wonder if maybe
I should sneeze again
> ~ jerry ball

nice to be blessed twice
but your heart stops beating
every time you sneeze!
> ~ nona

a few more facts
don't squeeze your nose, ear drums could burst
velocity:
one hundred and twenty-five
miles per hour!
goodness sake, just don't sneeze
if so, God bless you!
~ nona
for Carrie Nerheim

in between rains
blessed sunshine
warms our souls
~ nona

winter afternoon
two birds huddled on narrow branch
bracing against wind
~ nona

discarded poles
smiles lit up my face
happy am I...
~ nona

spring decorating
rearranging the front porch
with bamboo poles found
~ nona

the new year begins
when we realize we create
the times of our lives
~ nona

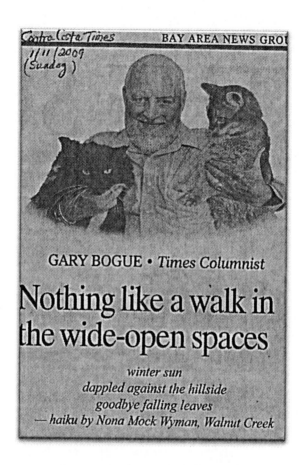

GARY BOGUE • *Times Columnist*

Nothing like a walk in the wide-open spaces

winter sun
dappled against the hillside
goodbye falling leaves
— haiku by Nona Mock Wyman, Walnut Creek

Gary Bogue with Nona's haiku

I know spring is here
for the weeds have grown
taller overnight...

> *my above haiku was GB's challenge*
> *for poets, to complete his 1st line -*
> *'I know spring is here...'*

this winter morning
the cold fog came drifting down
to splash in my face

> ~ Gary Bogue

across the sad sky
in a twinkling of an eye
seven stars went out
> ~ Gary Bogue
> *for the seven astronauts*

time to spring forward
and save some extra daylight
for taking a walk
> ~ Gary Bogue

why do mockers sing?
cause it's time to rock and roll
rock — mock — so much fun
> ~ nona MOCK wyman
> *for GB's annual 'mockingbird
> contest'*

when the world wearies
I find my sanctuary
my secret garden
> ~ nona
> *GB's request to compose a haiku for
> his 'Secret Garden' column*

dark clouds drifting in
from the sharp edge of the world
get snagged in tree tops
> ~ Lura Osgood
> *author*

the night tiptoes in
dark as trees full of shadows
silent as the moon
> ~ Lura Osgood

Jerry Ball holding his haiku on bark
in front of the Ming Quong store

(Article - Contra Costa Times/Walnut Creek Journal)

Jerry Ball, Past-President of the Haiku Society of America, Honorary curator of the American Haiku Archives at the California State Library in Sacramento.

'a light in the mouth'
is nature's fine spokesman
enlightening minds
　　　　~ nona
　　　　　for Jerry Ball

summer breeze
the honey bee holds on
for dear life
　　　　~ jerry ball
　　　　　author of numerous poetry books

spring rain
the hawthorn blossoms
draw into themselves
　　　　~ jerry ball

heavenly bamboo
bending under the weight
of the morning dew
　　　　~ jerry ball

friends exchange haiku
sending happy thoughts with love
shared a few brief words
            ~ Luanne Nieman

summer madness
'naked ladies' swaying
blushing pink
            ~ nona

called 'naked ladies'
my 'staid' sister said — now her bulbs
are in my garden
immersed in their fragrance
a favorite of mine
            ~ nona
                'tanka' for my sister, Ellen Nancy
                Ong's 'Amaryllis belladonnas'
                flowers.

breezy afternoon
strolling the garden
a hint of sunshine
            ~ nona

when life seems so bleak
a rose appears on the bush
a smile on my face
            ~ Sandra Miller
                cousin to Joe Wyman

though the flowers of fall
perish in winter's fierce cold
we will not forget

      ~ Kelley Kwong
        age 10, granddaughter of a Ming
        Quong Home alumna

oh my, much too hot
tuxedo cat flops down
like a worn out rug

      ~ nona

there's a cat
racing its
own shadow

      ~ Ryan
        4th grader

coming home
my neighbor's cat shuns me
its name, Scaredy cat!

      ~ nona
        for the Martin's cat

**"Scaredy Cat," impromptu sketch at the store by
Natalie Kwong, age 7 (Kelly's sister)**

on the mountain slope
ancient Buddha face — our cat
Jo Jo meditates...
~ nona
our 'tuxedo' feral cat

Two huge 'Sacred Stone' Buddha faces adorn our garden which
entranced our cat, Jo Jo. A card at our store states,
"I have lived with several Zen masters. All of them cats."
by Eckhart Tolle

'Maneki' – legend
the 'welcoming cat' waving
at many restaurants
~ nona
for Rachael 'Maneki' Kerkhoff,
whose Japanese heritage she
embodies, a former Ming Quong
employee

pretty clothes she sells
husband indulges, we buy
beautiful am I
~ Nana Brownell-Cope

Haibun

Part Two

Egyptian Earrings

One day at the store, the phone rang. It was Laurel Burch, the world-renowned jewelry-maker. Throughout the years we had become friends. She had once debuted her book at the store, shopped here and I had even introduced her to a new love or two! Men friends, that is!

That day her voice bubbled with excitement as she smiled into the phone and rippled joyfully:

"Nona I named an earring after you!"

Absolutely surprised I sucked in my breath and squeaked:

"You named an earring after me?" She giggled like an excited child reassuring me.

"You did?"
"It's an Egyptian flower."
"Really?"

I repeated, not quite believing what I had just heard. "What does it look like? I've never seen an Egyptian flower."

Laurel replied: "Neither have I."

We laughed so hard until, finally worn out from the excitement,

I came back to the present moment and thanked her with all my heart. The four Egyptian earrings were beautiful in half swirls, just like a mythical, exotic Egyptian flower! They were in shades of purple with red, red with black, gold with black and silver with black. Inscribed on the back of each drop earrings was Laurel's inscription:

'Ming Quong for Nona'

Reflections:

So many amazing 'flowers' in my life. It is awesome recounting these memories. Laurel was a one-of-kind person. She was ahead of me in the 'world of psychic.' Once on the phone we talked about

visualization. We proceeded to experiment on some subject which I now cannot recall now what it was. While visualizing the subject my hand holding the receiver suddenly became 'hot' and so did my ear! What was happening? At Laurel's end of the line in Sausalito it was not hot at all!

I looked around the store perplexed! Everything was normal, just my hand was hotter than hot, like I'd just pulled a hot dish out of the oven! I realized it was her amazing energy. In my world she was the most mystical artist I'd ever encountered.

Speaking of the world, when she visited China (which was before President Nixon's historical visit) she was so well-received that she gushed unabashedly that she paved the way for Nixon!

Laurel was our artistic ambassador!

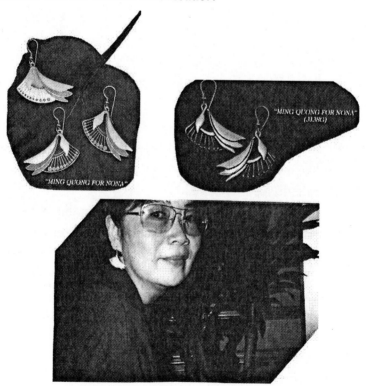

Nona with "Ming Quong for Nona"
earrings by Laurel Burch

The Image Of Love

compelling image
drawing the face of Jesus
summer contentment

It was the summer of 1968, the last evening of CFO (Camps Farthest Out), a non-denominational spiritual camp at Richardson's Spring in Northern California. While reminiscing with my friend Audrey about our week's experiences, my eyes fell upon a Jesus picture that instantly spoke to me and I felt this intense desire to capture the expression. It came with ease, the most satisfying charcoal portrait I'd ever done. (I had been commissioned in my thirties to draw charcoal portraits, which included a showing at the Kensington Library.)

Back at my Ming Quong store in Walnut Creek, I framed the black and white portrait, signed my name, 'Nona,' dated it, added CFO, and the word, 'Jesus' in Chinese calligraphy. Why I wrote Jesus in Chinese, I don't know, but it felt right. Maybe my Spirit moved me!

I walked joyfully across the street to the Bible Book Store and left it on consignment with the owner, a kind elderly woman. A week later the Jesus picture sold to a camp leader, a counselor at Boulder Creek. I was amazed at how quickly it sold. And was doubly surprised to hear how she specifically picked my picture foregoing traditional, well-known, Biblical faces of Jesus. She later shared:

lives were turned around
as youthful faces
felt the calling

And then an astonishing thing happened — the lanky, friendly red-haired man behind the counter spoke to me in Chinese! I was speechless! What was happening? Was I back at camp where I had witnessed a woman speaking in tongues for the first time? I remembered my reaction of confusion hearing her gibberish words! That scenario was all new to me! Now this man speaking Chinese confused me again. I realized he had picked up on my Chinese calligraphy of Jesus.

He was having fun with me! He shared how he as a child had been raised in China by missionary parents.

Amazing — my Chinese teacher, Mrs. Lee at the Ming Quong Home would have smiled broadly in her demure way. His Cantonese was perfect, far superior to mine!

> the following year
> Jesus featured on
> CFO's brochure

Reflections:

The following year, 1969, CFO asked if I would like to sell my drawing alongside their religious books. I was honored yet I hesitated as it didn't feel right to sell Jesus for a profit. I contemplated and decided I would if the drawing was sold as 'Love Offerings.' Meaning you contribute any amount you felt was right!

That was a positive learning lesson, seeing people's reaction to this method of buying!

> giving the love way
> came to mind from the spirit
> of CFO's teachings

Meanwhile back at the store, years later I ran across the extra Jesus picture from camp and pleasant memories surfaced. I mused, should I sell my Jesus drawing at the store? I did. They were sold as 'Love Offerings' also. How would my customers in the 'real world' react

to this method? They were pleasantly surprised. They embraced it.
Some couldn't believe it. They contributed from their hearts.

The Image of Love – Charcoal Sketch by Nona

*Then there was Kevin, Jim's employee who was astounded that I
had actually drawn the picture! He asked permission to take a picture
of it!*

*The proceeds benefitted Eastfield Ming Quong, known as, 'EMQ
Children and Families Services.' Eastfield was San Jose's first
orphanage, which combined with the Ming Quong Home orphanage*

many years later, after my time. They are now known as EMQ Families First.

The Ming Quong Home was sponsored by the Occidental National Board of Missions. Raised as Presbyterians, I learned about Jesus as a toddler in prayer time at the Home and at Sunday School and church.

> now embracing
> the goodness in all faiths and
> the spirit within me

Historical Facts:

The Bible Book Store was located where SuperCuts hair salon is now. Next door is upscale SaSa, a Japanese Restaurant where the well-known Lawrence Meat Market once sold the choicest meat in town. Historic signs and pictures of the 100-year-old meat market are preserved on the outside of the original brick building by Brian Hurihata, the owner, and past president of the Downtown Merchants Association.

A Starving Artist

Me, a starving artist? Not really, I like to eat too much! But one week-end I almost became one! My family and I were at one of our favorite places to explore, Sausalito. Joe had ordered one of my newly discovered sandwiches, a patty melt, plus some other delectable sandwiches from the grill for himself and Jim. Yum, I couldn't wait for our number to be called, which unfortunately took a while as this new hot spot was also popular with tourists. Meanwhile, Joe, in need of a good cup of coffee, opened his wallet and found only a few loose coins, barely enough for coffee!

a flat wallet
back then, no charge cards
no ATMs

In desperation we scanned the crowd and saw no one we knew, which was no surprise because we didn't know a soul in Sausalito at that time. Soon our number would be called. What should we do? The chef stepped up his pace grilling as fast as he could, as now two lines had formed close to our table. I was nervous, anticipating who-knows-what! And what should appear, a familiar face in line. A lone man who seemed hung over, and looked out of place. Who was he? We looked closely, and realized it was none other than Walter Keane, the famous artist known for his 'big eyes' on children's pensive faces. We knew him. But he seemed disoriented and so unlike the time we met him at his San Francisco studio in North Beach. That time his artistic appearance was a show in itself. I had fallen in love with his paintings and we had communicated well. In fact, after our visit he had given me a free poster, which Joe promptly framed, 'a-la-Joe style,' which meant molded strips of black wood (from a left-over project). Joe's touch was perfect. I loved it even more. It was my treasure.

That day in Walter's office I noticed a framed picture of a beach scene. I was surprised that he was the artist.

> a small colored
> painting of a stranded boat
> a different Walter!

This time I approached a different Walter. I had to do what I had to do: ask him for a loan.

> bewildered were we
> both of us lost beyond
> comprehension

But he heard my plea. I thanked him. That day we were saved by his grace, but I noticed he had left the line!

Reflections:

Thinking back to that scene and hearing about what happened to him after that Sunday, I hoped we did not make him 'the starving artist!'

Once when Joe was a process-server he had to serve divorce papers on our 'new friend' Walter Keane. Walter understood. Then sometime later — headlines in the San Francisco newspapers and Herb Caen's column pointed out that the famous artist was destitute! All his mementos were to be sold at the Danville Hotel to raise funds for him! With a heavy heart we attended the sale.

Joe bought a small hand-carved 'figa' capped with etched silver with an old-world look. Today this artistic piece hangs in my gallery at home, a gift given to Walter by the much acclaimed actress of the day, Kim Novak, whom I enjoyed at the movies.

Interesting how we are connected, as later I spoke to Lucile Hanford, a woman from my spiritual Thursday morning group who was a friend of Walter's ex-wife. She elaborated how Walter's wife was actually the official painter of the 'big eyes.' The Courts later verified this. The Walter I knew had a kind soul, an 'artist of the heart.' Today I enjoy my collection of both the Keane poster and cards regardless of who the painter was. These works speak of learned experiences, and is also a reminder of how other artists looked down on Walter, as a non-dedicated artist! It was a good 'Education in the Arts.'

The day I wrote this haibun was the same day 'Entertainment Tonight' interviewed Margaret Keane, who was then seventy-eight, on a forthcoming movie about life with Walter and all their tribulations.

At home next to the Keane artworks is a haiku I had composed...

> infamous 'keen' eyes
> which 'Keane' was the true artist?
> Walter, Yes ? No, Margaret...

Today my haiku is:
> keen eyes
> speaks to me
> of life's mysteries

Later, I finally saw the movie, 'Big Eyes' on DVD. It left me with a sadness. I took from the movie a sense of empathy and more awareness of human frailties. 'Big Eyes' jogged memories of growing up at the Ming Quong Home when my nickname was, 'Big Eyes.' This brought to mind Joe's gentle grandmother, who every time she saw me would smile and take both my hands gently and look lovingly into my eyes and say 'my eyes mirrored my soul.'

In the 'Big Eyes' movie that particular saying was also used!

That day in line with Walter, a life's scenario was played out; both our eyes mirrored our souls!

Burma-Shave

days of old
highway signs kept you amused
now, blasting billboards

Remember the long drives on a quiet country road where the Burma-Shave signs made you smile? Their off-beat humor of four or five sayings on separate signs kept the driver alert to catch the very last sign. And when you read it, you realized of course that it was a good-ole Burma-Shave ad! Burma-Shave, the face cream for men in a big blue jar. Now, the crowded freeways are crammed with oversized billboards you can read blocks away. No need for an eye chart! But these billboards still do their job, perking people up with a smile or two.

And then on other roads all kind of directional signs point this way and that. One example – coming off the San Mateo Bridge. That evening a carload of us from Walnut Creek was on the way to the Fremont library for my book reading. Lissa was ready to turn left off the bridge when I spied the lighted billboard to the right and gulped! What did I see? Not a regular advertisement, but words saying:

Nona Mock Wyman — reading tonight from her *Chopstick Childhood* book!

"Lissa, look, stop, wait!"

"I can't," she hollered.

Looking back at that ultimate surprise, I never thought it would happen again. But it did, this time in the small town of Moraga, close to St. Mary's College. In their shopping area a towering marquee featured my reading for *Chopstick Childhood*. I was thrilled, as I thanked the store owners. What a way to start off a reading in a new area or any place on this planet!

Then in 2013, another happening:

Danville Boulevard
Alamo's Women's Club
Nona Mock Reading

That official-looking blue sign by the road next to the Alamo's Women's Club had Linda Kwong, (my driver) blurting out, "Did you see that sign?" Like Lissa, I caught just the corner of the sign as we turned into the parking lot. But after parking, we walked backed and stared at the sign in astonishment. I found out later that a poet friend, Chris Horner, was on Danville Boulevard, saw the sign and nearly ran into a tree! But that sign convinced her to come to my reading!

Reflections:

Not really realizing what I was doing I believe these surprises came because of my belief system. I was open to receive the goodness of anything and everything. One of my 'Nona-isms' is:

Seeing everything in Divine Order

no matter what the situation is.

'Nona-ism' is a word coined by my good-friend, Lissa.

Linda Kwong is the daughter of my close friend Beverly from MQ days.

Cock-A-Doodle-Do

a rooster am I
waking up early each morn
just like my sign

One day I was with my North Main Street friends, Lissa, owner of the Main Source store across the street from my store and her two employees, Carol Lutz and Mary Spivey. I was planning my big '6—OH!' birthday party and I wanted a unique 'rooster' invitation to 'cock-a-doodle-do' everyone to come to my party! I happened to mention that my house needed a good cleaning job. And what did Lissa's mind conjure up? As only Lissa could do! She, along with Carol, literally cleaned my house until it shone like new...

floored beyond words
lucky me – lucky Joe
they were tuckered out!

Mary, a teacher/artist who lived in Berkeley, did something else, she commissioned herself to draw the party invite!

"Really?"....
she smiled
I waited

She produced the greatest rooster drawing I'd ever seen, complete with me as a rooster and even wearing my bothersome glasses. I loved it.

plumes of feathers
fanned my back as I crowed
"Cock-a-doodle do!"

Invitations were sent. One to March Fong Eu who at that time was the Secretary of State for California. March could not attend, but in her own way she replied in a 'stately-fashion' as only a politician in her position could do — she proclaimed:

A "Nona *Harken* Day"

for all Californians to celebrate my birthday!

disbelief —— 'a
proclamation with the Seal
of California'

This official surprise was awesome. Impressed, Joe had it framed and proudly insisted that I share it with everyone!

for Californians
honoring their request
front window at the store

On the party day (unbeknownst to me) my smiling neighbor, Carol Martin, had the proclamation in hand and shared it with the party-goers as they arrived!

glancing sideways
self-consciously
I moved out of sight

Later at the party, Mark Izu, a musician, suddenly blew some soulful notes from his Japanese instrument and everyone became quiet. What was happening?

That's when the 'perfect hostess' of the day, Eta Morris coolly announced a surprise.

The appearance of an unexpected guest who had flown in at the last minute—just in time for the party. We wondered, 'who was that?' And then we gasped:

as heads turned - it was
Rhoda — dressed as a Rooster!
'cock-a-doodle-do'

Reflections:

Rhoda was a former Ming Quong gal. We were roommates after the Home in Oakland. She was a wonderful friend, helpful and full of gumption. Her colorful (borrowed) costume was a hit.

The gourmet lunch that day was what dreams are made of!

The 'Chefs of the Day' were the two cousins, Jim Wyman and Clay Headley who expertly grilled the brined chicken and savory pork ribs perfectly. Brian Murphy, the sharp photographer, was catching all the action.

'Everybody' and 'everything' made this story of my life unforgettable.

Lasagna In India

yum yum
dishing up lasagna
I think of Mama

In the 1980s I met an India woman with a persona that exuded ancient beauty. Her flowing silk saris were a delight to my eyes. I took a liking to her instantly. Some people are like that.

She was Lissa's mother-in-law. She had a name I couldn't pronounced, so I simply called her 'Mama' because Ash (her son) called her Mama, which of course was what he'd always done. But when I heard 'Mama' spoken from him, it was so endearing and affectionate, it made me realize what I had genuinely missed in my life. Mama loved me calling her Mama and so did I.

She was always curious about everything. So one Sunday she accompanied me to the Apparel Show in San Francisco. She reveled in everything, especially conversing with the East Indian vendors. But what she enjoyed the most was something she loved with a passion. Food! This discovery at lunch time changed her family's palate back in India. Bon Appétit, the celebrated caterer of that era, was serving lasagna and that intrigued her. I was concerned for her as all the seats were taken, the only place available were the low stairs. But she managed beautifully, graciously gathering her long sari beside her.

Savoring every bite she asked a multitude of questions. I smiled at her enthusiasm.

scrutinizing
every layer
she had it down pat

We ate with gusto. In fact she contemplated seconds!

Back in Walnut Creek, she raved about it to Lissa and Ash. Back home in India, she experimented and the lasagna was a huge success. The family devoured it. Whenever she visited Ash and Lissa, she would whip up all her Indian dishes for a large group of us...

I smiled
envisioning Mama — the
Oneness of it all

Plain Jane

Plain Jane was no plain Jane! She was Jane Stone, known as JStone. She was an accomplished award-winning card-maker, featured at the Smithsonian Institute, plus a fine jewelry maker. Her cards were well-liked by celebrities such as John Denver, who, before his death, had sent a JStone card. Also, Hillary Clinton is a fan; plus, of course, all my customers who are tuned into her heart-warming sayings and her hand-painted art on each card. My customers have made JStone the 'best-selling' card line in my store. Her cards, stamped with a Chinese signature chop, intrigued me. Who was this woman?

> throughout the years, my
> Chinese accent turned JStone
> into, Jade Stone

Try saying her name out loud? JStone? Sound like Jade Stone? Say it again quickly! Anyhow, after a few years it begins to sound differently; a lesson in English/Chinese annunciation! I also noticed that the back of the card included: 'One JStone Plaza' That piqued my interest. Then one day there was an error on the order, so I called and asked, "Who's this?"

It was JStone in person, the woman I so admired. I blurted and gushed, "It's you, I can't believe it. I love your meaningful cards, in fact, everyone loves your cards!"

She laughed, a wholesome hearty sound, emanating from the depth of her soul. I liked her instantly. As we talked, I felt a rapport from ages past, like someone I had grown-up with at the Ming Quong Home orphanage! But of course that was not a fact! Like a good friend from the 'Home,' I felt I could talk to her about anything. So I asked her two questions that had been in my mind all these years.

"Are you rich or something?"

"Why?" she laughed.

"Because your business is located in JStone Plaza."

"Oh that," she humbly and laughingly put down was because it was:

an honor bestowed
by Silverton, Oregon
for my talent

Impressed by her humility, my second question was, "what is your first name?"

"Jane."

"Jane, is that all?" I screamed. "Just Jane!" I repeated in disbelief.

"Yes, why?"

"Because I always thought your name was Jade. See, try saying JStone," I lamented. Then, in a stupid stupor I asked, "Wouldn't you rather be called Jade?"

Her answer, more laughter.

Anyhow, plain ole Jane was certainly not plain Jane! When she found out about my book, *Chopstick Childhood*, and how I was an orphan, she nearly exploded! Then when she told me she was an orphan also, I nearly exploded!

And so we talked extensively about our experiences. She shared how she had been adopted by a well-to-do banker family, who neglected her. One story concerned her tattered shoes and how both soles were completely split and flapping. But her parents were unconcerned and didn't really care! So Jane took it upon herself to find the prettiest ribbons around and tied the soles together and topped it off with a big bow! And Jane bubbled over with more laughter.

What a gal! Her life experiences are expressed in her cards. We made a trade; some of her cards for my *Chopstick Childhood* book. At this point, Jane said we are 'soul sisters,' and I agreed.

Reflections:

To find out more about my 'soul sister' Jane, please read 'Buddha Face.'

Buddha Face

Jane Stone sent accolades my way after reading my book, *Chopstick Childhood in a Town of Silver Spoons.*

> expect a surprise soon
> she happily informed me
> I couldn't wait

The package arrived, a unique, classy JStone gift box. Inside, layer upon layers of contrasting pastel tissue paper. It was like a box full of fluffy clouds at sunrise.

> opening the box
> I gasped – a face necklace
> instant love

How did she know? I've always loved faces, and all my life I had always drawn faces, mostly of women. Now here was this beautiful pendant. On the phone Jane apologized for the unfamiliar face. But she said the image was me! It was created from her memory from my book which she had loaned to a friend.

It was awesome. "It was ME!" I exclaimed, not once, but twice!   Her inscription on the back of the box spoke of our unique store and our oneness as soul sisters. She named the pendant, the 'Nona necklace' to honor my *Chopstick Childhood* book.

Nona Necklace by Jane Stone

I loved it so much she made fifty limited editions of 'Nona.' My customers loved it also.

> people observed
> a meditative Buddha
> 'no, it's me — Nona!'

Every day I wear my 'Nona' necklace, Jane's love is felt, while Buddha's serenity surrounds me.

Reflections:

Throughout the years Jane created nine necklaces for me! All masterpieces. When not worn they adorn several walls alongside photos and framed pictures, accenting the area as art pieces. Each piece tells a story. One for a birthday, some for the special holidays and one fun pendant with a frothy sundae bead for when I truly want to indulge and have fun!

But one extra-ordinary necklace is hung next to my 'royalty' picture. It is my mother! Yes, my mother, a face I could not recall. Yet, with no pictures of my mother, Jane had produced a necklace! One evening Jane had been working late and suddenly a vision appeared before her. Instinctively she knew it was my mother. And right away she created my mother's face.

The 'art of patience' tested me! When the package arrived, I held my breath and what did I see?

I beheld a familiar face; looking closer I saw my sister's image! It was amazing as all my life my relatives had always told me 'your sister looked like your mother.'

> soul sister's lesson
> in another dimension
> awesome wonderment

Double Meaning

once upon a time
in a land where spinsters ruled
a girl's orphanage

Always thought it'll be fun to start a story with, 'Once upon a time,' because it seemed like it would be a 'fantasy' type of story! So I did, but with a different twist, I used a haiku! And the story goes...

Many moons ago in a far-off-place known as Ming Quongland, this little toddler named Nona came to live. It was a fun place to grow up, far away from city life. She was the youngest with an innocence inherent in her!

When she was in her teens, she was still quite naïve; the older girls nicknamed her, 'Greenhorn!'

She landed in Walnut Creek and ran a store called Ming Quong. It was here she learned many 'grown-up' lessons in life. For example, she sold many different stones, some with meaningful, positive sayings like, 'Everything Counts be Thankful,' 'Blessed Be' and more. In her collection there was one rather large stone which always elicited laughter. It was etched with, "Please Turn Me Over," and on the back it read, "Thank You."

Nona had a lot of fun joking with her customers about the 'polite rock.' They'd smile more, often times chuckling.

Then one day a siren of a woman came in with a friend and picked up the stone and with a gasp she let out a thunderous laugh right before Nona's eyes!

she rocked the store
screaming, "this is too funny"
they roared till they ached

And a startled Nona wondered why. She continued to stare at this flamboyant woman and it suddenly dawned on her, this rock had a double meaning!

That day Nona learned a whole lot more about life!

Reflections:

Seriously, Ming Quongland, actually named 'Ming Quong Home' was not a fantasy. It was, as one alumna said, a "Ripley's Believe or Not" scenario which existed in Los Gatos, California. Back then, this 'far-off-land' once housed Chinese orphan/needy girls. If you haven't already, check out this little-known history, it is captured in:

'Chopstick Childhood in a Town of Silver Spoons'

This 'silver spoon home' was once owned by the Spreckels Sugar family, who lost this summer home during the Great Depression of the 1930s.

Really?

Should I write this or not? Because I can't believe it happened. My mind says, yes, because 'it's reality.'

This happened — when I was an adult 'Greenhorn!'

'Greenhorn' was my nickname at the Ming Quong Home when I was a teenager. Given my upbringing at the orphanage, I was perhaps the most naïve storeowner on North Main in suburban Walnut Creek, California!

Back in the early 1970's, the Ming Quong store carried the first cut-out garments in Contra Costa County. Known as krawang, this intricate work from Bali was reminiscent of lace work. It was thick colorful threads embroidered around the cutout design. It was the most feminine artwork to hit the Bay Area. One of our popular krawang items was a summer outfit, a white camisole with wrap-a-round shorts. It had delicate pink flowers and embroidered leaves.

Customers loved these creative pieces.

One morning at the store in walked a tall, lanky guy with black heavy-rim glasses. He had a tangle of long dark brown hair and needed a shave. His eyes behind his rimmed glasses protruded like a frog. He was nervous. And like a frog he leaped over to the camisole and shorts sets & asked to try them on. I was speechless.

Before I could utter a reply he darted into the dressing room.

Back then there were no mirrors in the dressing rooms so he used the large mirror in the store. Out he came & asked how he looked. I had never seen a guy dressed like a woman and I was again speechless. My eyes didn't blink while he pivoted in front of the mirror. It was obvious he liked his image! What was happening? Was this for real? I don't know if I was embarrassed or what!

Back into the dressing room he went. He seemed to take a while, but he finally emerged dressed in his street clothes and without a word he zoomed out the front door.

What a relief, and so fortunate there was no one else around! I checked out the dressing room and found the outfit in disarray. The top was clipped haphazardly – and the wrap shorts were dangling from one tie narrowly missing the floor! What a mess.

But what was worse when I went to straighten out the shorts, a milky white substance oozed onto my fingers! I couldn't believe it. He had masturbated!

"Really?" — Yes, really.

> first and last ever
> how to prevent it again
> it never happened!

My education was forth-going! One of my mottos was 'to learn something new every day.'

And I did!

And now the second — 'Really?' story, now this one was a 'clean' act!

Clothes had been disappearing from the store. No likely suspect. But someone had 'good taste!'

Then one time I was in Jim's side of the store when my front door on my side of the store opened with a loud thud and the bells on the door jangled extra loud. I dashed over quickly through the archway to my side as this person sounded urgent; but I was surprised to find no one around. It was strangely quiet. Like no one had entered. But yet the bells were still vibrating.

I looked in the dressing room and what I saw puzzled me! Two pieces of clothing were hanging in the room which had not been there before.

I surveyed the apparel and realized they were the garments which had been stolen! They had been returned with their respective hangers! I was stunned. It was like they had never left the premise.

And I wondered why...

> it didn't fit
> maybe worn once, or perhaps
> feeling guilty!

Reflections:

These 'Really?' stories are fortunately not as prevalent. For me, my 'education in life' was sharpened by the realities of human behavior.

God's Hand At Work

It was 2014 when Dave Kwinter, a man with a pleasant smile and a rather mischievous look, strolled into the store plunked his bag down on the floor with a thud and asked me to be a speaker for the Kiwanis Club.

I hesitated. Why? Who knows? But he was different. It was probably his off-way of asking, as if comprehending a 'whatever' reply!

My reply — a few moments of silent perplexity! Who was this man? He triggered my curiosity! I had been on the reading circuit since 1998, with many gratifying presentations that by now the invitation to read was a rather natural occurrence, although I was always in awe and amazed when people asked me to speak.

So that day, I asked Dave where their group met, how many people attended and just inundated him with no-nonsense questions, like, why do you want me to read to your group and how long will I be there? He eloquently answered each question with flair and he concluded, "Lunch will be included!"

"Yay," I replied, and mischievously teased, "What else?" Poor Dave had no reply. That's when I related my reading experience in Los Gatos and how that Kiwanis Club served a hearty breakfast and gifted me with a neat Kiwanis mug.

"Hmm, maybe I can find a mug!" Dave replied.

I quipped, "No mug — I don't think I'll do it!" Of course he didn't believe me! After tons more laughs we were like old-friends from way-back-when. It was evident from the beginning what my reply would be:

> I always say, "Yes"
> Ming Quong is a part of me
> I can't say, "No"

And this "Yes" to Dave became one of the most uplifting venues I'd ever attended! For example:

Kiwanis met
right behind my store
how good was that?

The Massimo restaurant happened to be one of my favorite spots. A customer from fifteen or twenty years back was formerly the chef there; his meat sauces spooned over the entrée were heavenly! So I was already excited! And I could go there on my own, no one had to drive me. It was perfect!

Upon entering — the room was charged with joyous laughter from the happiest/friendliest people I'd seen in a long time. Some were familiar-looking. My customers? One man in particular, Jim Cole, was our customer. A tall man with a gregarious personality and the brightest smile. Now grown-up, he possessed the same charm he had when he was a teenager and he would come buy jewelry for all his girlfriends!

reminiscent
of a Ming Quong reunion
I was amongst friends

But I'm ahead of my story! That day my good friend, Paul Lee, and his daughter, Pam, came to visit me at the store. We always had lunch out and today was my treat, so I invited them to the Kiwanis 'event.' They were welcomed immediately as 'their' guests! I told Dave kiddingly if I had known that, I would have invited more people!

We sat with Dave. People were trooping in and soon all the seats would be filled. Dave kept telling me, "It is because of you." I didn't believe him. And when they had to set up another table, I believed him. During lunch time, more surprises; the president of the club, Cherice Gillam, is an Eastfield Ming Quong employee. So similarities were felt. Precision was the keynote, just like being back at the Ming Quong Home. I was to talk only for a specific time period and to make sure I understood she would let me know! And she placed a clock in front of me! That reminded me of the 'bell system' that was rung at the Home for each event of the day. My upbringing kicked in, I was precise, with a few minutes to spare, although I felt flustered as I had to leave out some information.

I must have been okay, because at the end of the session, Cherice asked me if I would do a reading at EMQ!

That day I met an inspiring man, Reverend Robert Williams, known as Reverend Bob, a retired Presbyterian minister who was in his 90s. He had unlimited energy for taking care of all the necessary things active members did, like making sure all name tags were displayed and in order; and to his credit he was also like a waiter or busboy who was here, there and everywhere. He even swept the floor! What a tribute to his ministry. His manner of dress was also smart and impeccable.

> kidded about
> being a man-of-the-cloth
> his ears were turned off

Yes, he was kidded just like we did at the 'Home' but of course we never had a smiling Reverend Bob to joke around! Most all our women teachers on the staff were stern and besides there were no men teachers around in my era, but if we had, he would have been a good role model!

He knew the entire history of the 'Home.' He also knew my friend, the late Frank Mar, and his wife, Mary (a former MQ gal). Frank Mar had been the minister for the Presbyterian Church in Oakland, next to Chinatown, which us MQ girls had attended.

He sat next to Pam, who herself is an elder at the same church. Amazing, God's hand was at work.

Next to me was my good moral supporter, Paul, who calls himself my 'banker,' who once helped me with sales of my book at the Chung Mei/Ming Quong reunion, and here he was doing it again!

Then, after the flag salute, a most reverent moment happened for me when Reverend Bob stood up to offer his prayer:

> all heads bowed
> familiar words came forth
> and – I was home...

A glorious, fulfilling day. And to top it off Dave surprised me with a Kiwanis mug!

Reflections:

The Kiwanis chapter/haibun continues in 'Kiwanis Helping Hand'. The Kiwanis organization helps children worldwide.

To know more about Paul Lee, please read, 'Husband In Name Only.'

The Kiwanis 'Helping Hand'

At age eighty-one I learned something new about men!
Something nice! Something comforting.

After my talk at the Kiwanis book reading I limped out of
Massimo's to head back to the store. Dave Kwinter noticed and
extended his arm and simply said, "Here, take my arm – it may help."
I did and I was back to normal. My walking was perfect! *What a
revelation, what a gentleman.*

>   like 'offering hands'
>   it does wonder
>   for the soul

A few days later Pete Schmitt, the Kiwanis secretary came in with
a meaningful thank-you letter, their colored brochures and an
invitation to join the group. I was grateful, but not being much of a
joiner and because of my situation I didn't reply.

Then two separate emails, in part, said:

>   you're invited
>   on any Tuesday
>   to be my guest

They were from Dave Kwinter and Jim Cole. It left me speechless.
Two generous offers, I was tempted! Then came the holiday season
and a Christmas party invitation from Dave and his girlfriend Shirley.

>   can you hear
>   the echoes
>   of joy?

After the Kiwanis reading my ears were tuned into any perspective speakers for the group. I've invited four great people who happened to be Ming Quong customers. Musician Terry Horner, author Ron Lew and Timothy Hamilton, a youth counselor. And Dr. Al Loosli, a beloved sports doctor for the Walnut Creek Aquanauts, and former Olympics stars.

With each acceptance I've joined them and the group for lunch. Am I blessed or what? I've also attended several other meetings when a featured speaker captured my interest. So far they've all fit into my schedule.

I feel great, I feel enlightened and I get to see my new friends where I am fortunate to once again laugh and joke with the happiest group in Walnut Creek.

Their new co-presidents, Dirk Fitzgerald and Don Arington add their jovial enthusiasm to the group. Meanwhile the past-president Cherice Gilliam, is now the Governor-elect of the California, Nevada and Hawaii Kiwanis International. Cherice is the first African-American woman president for the Walnut Creek group and for the CaNevHi International.

History enacted right before our eyes. 'Congrats to all' — and for Eastfield Ming Quong also.

At my last meeting when I previewed my third book, the session ended with a gong. The president had actually struck their Kiwanis bell which at each meeting was always centered on the table. I had missed seeing him strike it, but I heard it clearly and was entranced. No one had ever rung it at the other sessions!

It was like a tranquil moment, like a sign of hopefulness, perhaps for this new book!

Keeper Of The Secrets

Buddha meditates
but the white face deeply etched
is she troubled?

In my store there is a large framed photo of myself pictured with a bigger than life Buddha's face behind my back. This surprise gift was given to me by Lani Phillips, a professional photographer and is titled, 'Keeper of the Secrets.' The photo in black and white is fascinating with my face as white as snow and only one color left in the photo, the red design on my blouse.

Lani is the creator of the Wise Woman boxed cards and a former Ming Quong store customer. Her title for my photo was perfect! For at that time I was actually a keeper of the secrets as I was writing the *Bamboo Women* book, about the lives and secrets of the Ming Quong women.

It took ten years to write that book and during that time their secrets burdened me, it was hard! In 2014 at the San Francisco's Cameron House 140th anniversary we toured the premises. Down in the basement we saw the underground coal bins where the rescued slave girls had been hidden from their kidnappers. Then upstairs in the game room, next to the stairs leading up to the fifth floor, I spied under the stair well an inconspicuous safe built right into the wall, nicely hidden.

This wall safe had amazingly survived San Francisco's devastating earthquake. The safe was now painted Chinese red blending in with the décor of the game room. It was definitely big enough to hide volumes of important documents!

but the key was lost
generations of lost truth
important secrets?

That day I was talking with Brenda Wong Aoki, a performing artist and storyteller. She was the daughter of a Ming Quong woman. Brenda's two uncles had lived at the Chung Mei home (for needy boys.) Brenda had many unanswered questions about her family as to why members of her family looked so different from each other. She was overjoyed that I acknowledged this as I was the only one who had ever agreed with her!

throughout her career
threatening stares cast her way
stopped her voice

I knew her frustration as my cousin had the same question about his brother. As an adult he heard the truth from my half-sister.

arranged marriage
true love cast aside
infidelity

Finally my cousin's secret was acknowledged. He felt validated, the truth bought relief. I felt Brenda's anguish and dilemma. It seems the foremost Asian storyteller of our time will have to wait to tell the story. And I wonder what does this unshakeable, everlasting safe contain?

I would say it is truly the 'Keeper of the Secrets!'

Reflections:

The day the photo, Keeper of the Secret, was taken for the Wise Woman's boxed cards, Lani realized it didn't fit the project's theme, as I was in the Grandma category! But blessed was I, as I, the Keeper of the Secrets for the Ming Quong women reaped this unique photo for myself and my store customers.

> behind the white face
> few secrets never disclosed
> are locked within me!

Notes:

Cameron House, located in San Francisco's Chinatown was a rescue 'mission home' for needy women in the 1900s.

The bigger-than-life Buddha face is an award-winning waterfall fountain, two doors from Ming Quong at the Modern China Café restaurant. It was created by the former owner, John Hung Le of the 'Three Seasons Restaurant.' In the early years this 'historic house' with its expansive lawn and a towering walnut tree housed Walnut Creek's first medical doctor.

Update to 2016: Did you catch the TV milk commercial with Steph Curry, the Warriors' MVP basketball star at the Cameron House? He was in the heart of Chinatown using their basketball court with a grand view of the SF skyline! Exhilarating. But on the 'contract' no one was allowed to talk to him. No press, absolutely nobody! But the kids at CH couldn't resist and out of their mouths came happy, "Hi's" :)

Nona with Buddha Face

When You Become As Little Children

The above title is a partial Bible verse engrained in my mind since my religious upbringing as a child memorizing Bible verses at the 'Home.' The verse bought back memories of Rhoda Wing, a former Ming Quong woman who had two adorable grandchildren who were models for the designer/company, Don't You Want to Peek?

Pictures of them modeling were hung in her living room. One particular picture which was used in a calendar was my favorite. It was her youngest granddaughter, Dylan, relaxing outdoors draped over a fence with the sweetest smile. I asked and bugged Rhoda for it as she had two copies of this picture. Rhoda was uncertain as her daughter Lisa had given it to her before the actual calendar was produced. But Rhoda could see I was in love with the picture and finally relented with a bright smile on her face, just like Dylan's smile!

The first time Dylan and I truly connected was at the store, when she was two and a half years old. After an impromptu lunch next door, munching on a hot-dog dripping with ketchup, she asked me between mouthfuls:

"Would you like to come to my birthday party?"

Oh my gosh, I felt my heart melt. How cute was that? In my heart I knew that was not feasible, but thoroughly enjoyed the 'invite.' There were other sweet encounters.

Then several years later was the last time I saw Dylan, at Rhoda's memorial. She and her sister, Kaia were outside with us on the lawn observing the people in line, knowing what this service meant. They were restless in constant motion.

One woman looked their way and acknowledged them and said:

"Your Pau Pau (grandma) was a nice woman."

I held my breath hoping the two girls would be able to handle the moment. Dylan was silent for a second and replied:

"I liked her the most."

> absolute love
> the natural world of children
> a blessed relief

Reflections:

Today Dylan's picture (from Rhoda) hangs on my kitchen cupboard where it's right in front of me. There's no special wall for this precious picture because regular wall space is filled! But it's perfect right where it is. It's put up with a clear plastic cover held up by good-ole 'blue tak.' The picture energizes me and like a delighted child I'm always smiling!

> keep it simple
> become as little children
> spontaneous

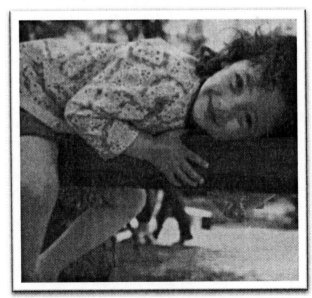

Dylan 'modeling'

The Night The Sky Exploded

child cringes
reassured by her parents
she breathes again

It was the fourth of July and the above scenario touched my heart. I felt the child's fear as I once experienced her pain. But I was not a child when it happened; I was in my early teens when we older girls at the Ming Quong Home in Oakland were invited to a Doctor Yee's home in Sacramento. The doctor was the father of a daughter who boarded at the Home while she attended medical school.

It was to be a full day, first to view the State Capitol, then to enjoy an outdoor Chinese buffet and attend the evening's festivities, which were a secret! We couldn't wait. Even the teachers smiled in anticipation. The plush lawn crowded with people sat quietly like perfect silhouettes, their faces pointing upwards. We found a knoll and settled down. And then it happened...

the sky exploded
spitting fire rained — I cringed
would I burn to death?

Safe at Home, the other teachers asked, "How were the fireworks?"

I barely nodded
still numb with fear
no one ever knew

Uh-Oh!

What's it like to finally be at my first book reading and actually signing a book? After five years of 'solitary writing' the contrast was startling. Actually live people waiting for me to speak! It was:

> unbelievably
> daunting and completely
> exhilarating

I was at the park in San Jose at the Chinese Historical Museum. It was a beautiful Sunday afternoon. It seemed the entire Chinese community was out to celebrate the Year of the Dragon which included a parade featuring Amy Chow, the celebrated Olympic gymnast.

On the program were three authors with their new books. Judy Yung, the revered author of Chinese history and a professor at UC Santa Cruz, Gerrye Wong, the much-read columnist for Asian Week with her book featuring Chinese Seniors and myself reading and discussing *Chopstick Childhood*.

Each participant had their own separate time. For my reading there were about fifteen people. This included my sister Ellen Ong, family relative Ed Wong, my Aunt A-Wah and my Mock cousins. Also there that day some Ming Quong Home 'girls' and their husbands plus my family, Joe and Jim and a few other listeners.

> comforting to see
> upright faces truly
> listening!

The reading and question and answer period went well. Inspiring attendees thanked me for sharing my story. One woman was Kammy Rose, a former San Jose teacher who had been a volunteer at a booth that day. She had to get back to her station so we only exchanged a few words.

After the reading I went outside into the bright sun light where the soft breeze kissed my cheeks. That was comforting; in fact now that the reading was over with I could relax, and do what I love to do, 'people-watch'.

Walking with my group of supporters to my assigned booth, we saw a young girl waiting for me for my book! Pleased and smiling I asked her name. It was a common name like Laura, so I wrote 'To Lauri;' "Uh- oh!" I uttered. She smiled and politely replied, "It's OK!"

> apologizing
> I changed 'i' to 'a'
> face redder than red

After she left, I groaned to Jennie, an MQ gal, "My first one and I misspelled her name! How embarrassing!"

> Jennie understood
> for she was my 'twin sister'
> at the Home

A few weeks later I received a surprise letter from Kammy Rose. She had talked to the head librarian in San Jose and my *Chopstick Childhood* book was now in eleven libraries plus the Main Library. Unbelievable. The book at the Main Library would remain there permanently along with other historical books, not to be checked out but to be used only while at the library.

> proud for 'the teachers'
> fulfilling their mission
> of rescuing girls

Reflections:

Looking back—my 'first' day was a day of learning and gratefulness. Though fearful at first, now I'm more relaxed. When you speak from the heart, your experience will flow like a river of joy!

Not mentioned in the above haibun, I did learn that 'watching' was an important part of the scenario. For example, a senior woman was skimming through the book when without a word she suddenly turned away and took the book with her. Ellen and I were speechless. My older sister ran after her. She said, the woman thought it was free! What I derived from this episode was the obvious, be observant!

Just Do It!

Back in the mid-1960's, guitar playing was music to my ears and to be like Joan Baez would be heavenly. What a voice, uplifting, clear and inspirational; like an angel. So I bought a nice-looking used guitar with a good tone at the Alameda Flea Market for ten dollars, complete with a case.

Now I was ready! I tuned into PBS, channel 9 and took guitar lessons from Laura Weber once a week. With the first lesson, I was playing 'Skip to my Lou' with just two chords! Pleased, I was on my way! The only drawback? I couldn't tune the guitar! But that didn't deter me — I just asked a friend.

By about the fifth lesson, I had the confidence to take in students to supplement my husband's teaching income. I advertised in the Homeowner's newsletter that with only one lesson you could be playing the guitar. Eager students came forth. But the one criterion was they had to tune their own guitar before each lesson. They did!

That summer I attended a spiritual retreat for 'Camps Farthest Out.' The song leader, Eugene Jones, somehow knew I was singing and playing for the little children, as I was the assistant to Dorothy Olsen, the pre-school director. It was 1969, the year the first astronaut landed on the moon. So I had composed a simple song and taught the young ones the lyrics:

I thank God for the stars above, I thank God for the moon,

I thank God for the universe and for landing on the moon.

The children sang as taught. Nothing earth-shattering, just my first song written and sung! I was grateful Dorothy kept herself in the background as I had always been just a 'choir singer!'

But who knows what would have transpired had I been brave! At camp there was a special program for sharing. When Eugene asked me if we could sing a song together, I froze. What came out of me was a "No!"

I couldn't believe I said 'No' to this man whom I revered and, in my opinion, had the best bass voice around! But I felt inferior, a complete amateur and he would find me out! Not sure if Dorothy had told him about me and my guitar, but I was too self-conscious and didn't want to embarrass myself. I was upset with myself for days.

That offer from Eugene was unreal! It would have been the highlight of my CFO experience! How could I perform with such an awesome, musical man? He was the well-known music director for the Berkeley Community Choir who every Christmas performed The Messiah. He was compared to the great Paul Robeson and had appeared in musicals for Ole Man River and with his charismatic personality, he was a good spokesman for his race.

On sharing night, he sang a hymn with four women, 'How Strong a Foundation.' In my choice of religious songs, that hymn had no melodic notes to move me or lyrics to embrace me. As I listened to their seemingly mechanical voices, it left me listless like the song! No Joan Baez moment!

Just remembering this episode leaves me with a dull ache; I learned that 'saving face' was not worth it, just made me feel worthless!

live life — no regrets
just do it
you will love yourself!

be grateful, thankful
you have the choice to say, 'yes'
to life's surprises

Reflections:

Years later, some of my young eager students happily came to the store and told me how they entertained at convalescent homes and performed at different venues. I was pleased. They had followed their 'love.'

A Husband In Name Only

It was 2003, and the largest reunion was happening for the Ming Quong and Chung Mei Homes, at the Legendary Palace Restaurant in Oakland's Chinatown. Over 250 people attended, including relatives and friends.

At our table were many Ming Quong 'girls' along with my good friends, Darlene and Paul Lee. Darlene grew up in Chinatown and lived there all her married life and was known as the unofficial 'Mayor and Historian of Oakland Chinatown.' She knew everything and everyone one connected with that area. Chinatown was well-represented!

Some other attendees there were Jeff Chan, a former Mr. Chinatown who came by our table particularly to acknowledge his old girlfriend, Carol, an MQ gal and my 1st playmate at the Home. Many people said 'hellos' which included our retired minister, the late Paul Lee who was active politically. Exhilarating to see so many diversified and smiling people!

During dinner, there were presentations. I spoke about living at the Ming Quong Home and then I unexpectedly had the MQ gals come up on stage to sing 'Jesus wants me for a Sunbeam,' a song we loved at the Home. That left us giggling like only MQ gals can do, especially when we goofed! Darlene particularly enjoyed our 'crazy' behavior!

After the full banquet, I strolled the room and spied one of the most popular Oakland men around — he had lived kitty-corner from the MQH on Ninth Street. In his youth he had always reminded me of a Chinese Frank Sinatra, slim and suave. He had dated quite a few of the MQ girls. This evening he was charming as ever.

I motioned him over and surprised him as I draped my arm around his shoulders and walked him over to our table. Standing before Darlene and Paul, I grinned and asked, "Have you met my husband?" They were taken back, their mouths dropped and no words came forth. Their expressions tickled my insides!

> what's with Nona
> everyone knows he's married
> what is she up to?

I continued emphatically, "This is Wyman, my husband." SEE, I emphasized pointing to his name tag, which read, 'Wyman Chew' and pointing to my name tag, which read, 'Nona Wyman!' "See, we're married!"

Laughter ~ laughter ~ laughter.

After the reunion, two standing jokes continued, as one time Wyman knew Paul was 'BARTing' out to the store to see me and this suave ole Hollywood of a guy cracked, "Oh, you're going to see your girlfriend, huh?"

That's Wyman! And my reply to Paul for Wyman was, "Say hello to my husband!"

> what a reunion
> a husband and a boyfriend!
> only in real life!

Reflections:

Simply enjoy the moment!

Update — the years have gone by and sadly Darlene, Wyman Chew and Carol have passed away. Paul still visits about once a month and we do lunch. We reminisce. He's my connection to Oakland Chinatown. We have fun; I tease him about being my boyfriend. He replied once to a customer, "I'm younger than her!" Geez, how about that? Darlene would have been 'proud' of his remark as Paul had always been the quiet one! As for Wyman? Who knows!

The Mysterious Joe

Once, I spied a man's figure through the arch-way, on Jim's side of the store. He was quietly checking out cards. Who was this man? His age, his height and his unusually pale face made him stand out. I knew him from somewhere. Was it? Was it...?

Then Jim stepped through the archway and quickly blurted out that the man was none-other than Joe Di Maggio!

"Really? I thought so. Why didn't you tell me?" Jim had been too busy to let me know. That day he had escorted his grand-daughter to the store, as she was a regular customer. She shopped, while he browsed.

Darn, I missed my chance on meeting this celebrity of such high caliber! His persona always projected calmness, despite being the greatest baseball player ever and being married to Hollywood's most glamorous and famous actress—Marilyn Monroe!

But one thing that made me feel a little better was this fact:

Marilyn Monroe
cards were not displayed in the
section where he was...

I'm glad, for this man's love for his wife was well-known to the world, and I felt he would have been 'hurt' again. His heartache was absolutely filled with such grief.

Years later, when I became involved with raising funds for the Dean Lesher Regional Center for the Arts, I bid on a signed Joe DiMaggio baseball during a televised auction on TV and won! That was a first for me. All because he came into our store!

Reflections:

Of interest — what does the Mayor Rob Schroder of Martinez have in common with Joe DiMaggio and I?

Once I was a noon-time supervisor at the San Miquel Elementary School when Rob was a student. I noticed his 'all-American' looks, cute, blond hair, blue eyes and above all his good manners, and was impressed. He was a stand-out against some of the mischievous or unruly ones!

Sometimes I may mention to a customer from Martinez about their Mayor and I always speak very highly of him.

Now as Mayor he can proudly point out Joe DiMaggio's boat 'Joltin' Joe,' a nickname given him by his Yankee fans. DiMaggio gave this wooden boat as a keepsake to Martinez, his birthplace. The restoration for Joltin' Joe just garnered two awards at the South Tahoe wooden Boat Classic in 2015.

Ming Quong's Fashion Shows

Lucky me, there's a fashion show at the store, every day! That is, of course, when someone finds the perfect garments to try on.

I will then say to the customer, "Yay, try it on, I can't wait for the Fashion Show!" Most people laugh, and some chuckle in astonishment. Yes, they are 'the stars' and some light up with pleasure.

One in particular danced in pure enjoyment, watching her friend's attempts to find the perfect top for an extra special occasion. At the end, she helped her as she tried on an Asian top with a bamboo design, her friend had considered.

When we all looked at her, we knew instantly that it was the perfect one! Her face lit up and she became a changed person. We watched the star in her blossom, and that's when her friend danced her heart out! And to think that apparel wasn't even for her!

That special silk top was for a Chinese tea ceremony in Paris! The 'buyer' had never been out of the country, so she was a little overwhelmed. But, there's more to this story — all her expenses, travel, hotel, everything which included ten in her family would be completely paid for by her cousin—the bride, and her Chinese fiancé!

Another unforgettable fashion show was bound to happen—and it did, just not that day... as one day this woman came in and I knew her from somewhere. But, where? After talking to her, I decided she was the actress Louise Fletcher, who starred in 'One Flew Over the Cuckoo's Nest.'

But...

> I was wrong
> she was in fact
> Ellen Burstyn!

The famed Hollywood actress! Oh my — such an embarrassing moment! I apologized.

I told her brother, Steve, about my error. He shrugged it off, indicating others had done the same! He promised next time she was in town visiting her mother, he would bring her in again.

He did. Smiling, he stepped back to watch the interaction.

That seemed like a prelude for an unusual day at the store! It was. Ellen gravitated to the one-of-a-kind tie-dye outfits from 'Whispers,' a sixties company known for creating a sub-culture design and transforming them into classy mainstream apparels.

Ellen looked stunning in their creations. What a fashion show!

She was happy. I was happy; in fact all of us were smiling, which, of course included her great brother.

'red carpet' show!
each outfit a hit
she was the 'star'

Reflections:

Ellen Burstyn was an Academy Award Winner of 'Alice Doesn't Live Here Anymore' and runner-up for numerous other movies. The younger generation remembers her as the mother in the 'Exorcist.'

Whenever I view her in a movie, I smile. For many years, a colored picture of Ellen and her grand-nephew graced our 'customer gallery,' courtesy of her proud niece.

But, unfortunately after remodeling the store, the 'customers pictures' had to be removed.

Then, recently, in August of 2015, an 'original' MQ customer, Carlenne (who now lives out of state), came in and reminisced how she shopped here when she was a teenager. When she walked in, I was writing the finishing lines about the customer gallery for this haibun. She remembered the photo of Beth Toussaint, as she was one year behind her in school. We reminisced about Beth as a neat person, and as an actress, performing in 'Dallas' on TV, and the time she modeled our cut-out clothes (krawang), for the Contra Costa Times.

Those were the days of Lynn Carey, the popular and well-read fashion editor, and Dan Rosenstrauch, one of my favorite photographers! That fashion spread and an 8" x 10" picture of Beth, Betty Bethards, and Les Williams, along with other personalized pictures of customers, was like a special events tapestry wallpaper woven from their lives.

One picture featured a wedding, with the bridesmaids in their 'krawang' outfits.

each memory
each picture showcased
told a story

Visualizing

My second book, *Bamboo Women,* had just been published and I was in San Francisco Chinatown with my publisher, Chris Robyn of China Books and his wife, Josie, for the book reading at the library. We were inching along like a desert tortoise in the heart of Chinatown looking for a parking spot — which was non-existent. And I thought to myself, "Darn, I forgot to visualize the perfect parking spot!"

After circling the block a few times I spoke the words to myself, "The perfect parking spot is manifesting before us now." I half-heartedly told the two of them about visualization, as I was uncomfortable mentioning this, not sure what my publisher's reaction would be. They said nothing. Then on the next try we once again drove up and back down the same street and there it was, the perfect parking spot, right in front of the library! I was elated; the universe was watching over us, another spot appeared before we could even get into the first one!

> upmost importance
> one must believe
> it will happen!

Betty Bethards was the well-known person with this knowledge back in the 1970s. She was a psychic, dream interpreter and author. I would attend her lectures once a month in Walnut Creek at the huge Garden Room at Heather Farms, which would be jammed with people and many left standing.

Skeptic at first, I listened and was taken in by her presentation and down-to-earth personality. She always said, "Start small." I always thought 'parking' was big!

I passed this info on to some my customers who seemed 'open' and they'd come in elated, plus they'd tell me about their other successful visualizations.

The most recent one happened in 2014 when Jay, an East Indian man in his seventies whom I have been purchasing clothing for over thirty years, came to busy North Main Street for our appointment. That morning, concerned about Jay, I stepped out the front door and saw a car pulling into the perfect spot right before my store! Without my glasses on, I wasn't sure if that was him. But he waved and I smiled, once again amazed by the power of visualization!

Later I asked if he knew what visualization was; his assured reply was "Yes, I always pray." Hallelujah!

Betty was a great teacher, teaching me to always visualize a good-night's sleep with no disturbing dreams. It always worked. But, if I forgot to do it or was too tired... I learned my lesson!

> visualize — pray
> opens unforeseen doors
> life will be different

It's A Wonder

Step into Ming Quong, the smallest store on North Main in Walnut Creek where there are two stores hidden inside!

It's filled to the brim with merchandise. We were 1300 square feet originally, now we maintain a humble 550 square feet. Jim's store was next door. We had a breeze-way to cross over.

This change happened about twelve years ago, which made it easier for me to leave and give book-readings. Another bonus was, I was able to take a break, and just meander around and visit my neighbors. That was like a breath of fresh air.

One thing about owning and running a store is you never knew what would happen. For example, one day while reading the paper I read an article in the 'Local Section' of the Contra Costas Times that our store was named:

'Merchant of the Month'
headlines read, 'Forget Berkeley
Shop at Ming Quong.'

Fun! Especially to be compared to 'hip' Berkeley! I use to live in Berkeley and loved to explore their unique stores. Now years later here I was running a store comparable to Berkeley!

Carol Lutz, a Walnut Creek resident who has travelled the world, vehemently blurted, "Your store is better than Berkeley, it's the best of Berkeley!" The perfect compliment.

I remember one Spring day a group of young Japanese girls who were tourists stopped in front of the store. They looked up at the homemade Ming Quong sign and reread their directions. They turned to the person-in-charge and in broken English asked, "Is this the store?"

Assured by their leader, they quietly and respectfully looked around 'both sides' of the store. And soon excited smiles appeared followed by delightful squeals as they found treasures. At the check-out counter a challenge appeared as no one spoke English. But they did understand the dollar amount for each item.

The young women paid with 'traveler's checks.' Back then I had to make sure their name written in Japanese calligraphy matched their Japanese signature! It did, in fact it was actually simple to compare, thanks to many hours of Chinese School classes I attended while living at the Ming Quong Home.

With broad smiles and a slight nod they left our 'recommended store' very happy indeed. A wonderful experience for all.

Later a customer related, "When I have guest from out-of-town I always bring them here and to Nordie's. (Nordstrom.)"

wonderful
our store to browse and feel good
it's light beaming

Then one day a wonder to end all wonders happened! Joan Morris of the Contra Costa Times phoned and wondered if she could include our store in an article titled:

"Seven Wonders of the East Bay"

"Of course," I gasped! Not quite realizing at the moment the significance of such an honor. Exhilaration coursed through my body. Joan Morris was one of my favorite writers.

I remembered my question-mark response; I blurted out "Joan Morris? I love you!" Silence! And I continued on how I liked her various articles. She responded graciously.

The realization of this 'wonder' moment was real with me when Dan Rosenstrauch, the Times top photographer came in for a photo shoot.

Today, the full-page colored article hangs high on the history wall which happens to be a 'stairwell' leading upstairs to the guest rooms of the former Walnut Creek Hotel.

That slanted wall was the only space available! Sometimes a tourist will snap a picture of this article.

Reflections:

In my gift section, one of my favorite statues is 'Christ the Redeemer' standing tall with his arms stretched out over the buddhas and other gift items. When I chose this religious piece I had no idea that the statue represented one of 'The Seven Wonders of the World' located in Rio de Janeiro.

Like I keep saying, 'It's a wonder!'

'Ming Quong' and 'Christ
the Redeemer' — both
wonders in their way

What Happens After Eighty?

With no role model before me I sometimes wonder about new or unusual happenings! For example, when my left knee gave out at age eighty, no one told me I had used up all my cartilage! Besides, what's cartilage? I thought I had bumped my knee which I couldn't recall doing. It lingered for days and even Ben-Gay didn't help much.

Then when I fell and was laid up for over a month from the store, I found out my faithful knee had no cushion/cartilage left, it was now bone-on-bone!

What a lesson learned the hard way!

Have you seen those doctor/patient commercials on television where the questions are questionable? And the answers are, 'huh!' But my questions are of a different nature and should be more mature!

If I had my 'twin' sister Jennie here, we'd talked and compare life stories and laugh our heads off like teenagers at the Ming Quong orphanage. Especially as all but one of our live-in 'teachers' were spinsters. In her private Chinese way she was of no help. Any question hinting about the facts of life caused her cheeks to turn pink! Hopeless!

That's a hint of what it's all about — yes, the opposite sex!

Two pertinent questions are on my mind.

Do eighty year old women get proposals from men in their twenties? I can hear Jennie hysterically laughing while dabbing her tears and dubiously asking, "are you serious?"

> yes, I am
> yet wondering
> 'is this for real?'

Or am I over-exaggerating? Seriously, this is a pertinent question! My concerns for people are genuinely felt from the heart. Sometimes topped with 'Nona-isms' crowing like the 'Rooster' that I am!

'The proposal' happened next door at my Ming Quong store. I knew this likeable young guy for nearly three years. Handsome in the sense that he resembled a Greek God! Absolutely everyone young and old was drawn to him with his polite, personable ways. In passing he'd always ask me questions like, did I smoke, do drugs, or drink?

"NO."

In his mind he couldn't get over the fact that someone had such virtues! He'd constantly asked me 'to hang out' with him! And during the holiday when he received a 'free' turkey he repeatedly asked if I'd please come over and help him roast the bird as he'd never baked one. Ahh, how could one say 'no' to such a plea! But I did! But not without a slight smile in hopes of not hurting his feelings. Besides that was not me, fraternizing, and with a young one that I sensed was 'totally' on another planet!

To sidetrack him, I asked, "Do you like Jim's new employee?" Because like him, this one gal had many admirers. Everyone was smitten by her cuteness and demure ways!

"She's ok, but I don't know her like I know you."

Uh-oh, it was then I truly comprehended his fondness for me! And I began to feel uncomfortable and thought maybe I shouldn't talk to him so much.

But Life would be boring thinking like that! The fact about this Greek God was, everyone was always trying to fix him up.

One time Sal, our concerned substitute mailman, asked him if he'd met the girl working next door. Wrong question — tired of all these match-makers he turned to me and in front of everyone, proposed:

"Will you marry me?"

HUH! Now the question, was that for real? I was WOWED out, but in my 'Nona way' I answered:

> "YES — and you are all
> witnesses and invited
> to the wedding!"

No one spoke — the mailman was dumbfounded! I crowed like a rooster — or actually I was just being myself!

Later he realized my senior age. He mentioned it with a hint of what I perceived as annoyance. In retrospect, was he perturbed at himself or me? Maybe 'everyone!'

As for me, looking back, I felt a sense of regret at my 'cock-a-do' answer, hoping I hadn't hurt his feelings!

Memories are gentle and perhaps the scenario is off, but I will continue to be true to myself, with a smile for all, a caring heart for all, and above all, loving everyone unconditionally.

Did I just answer my pertinent question?

Yes, this sounds familiar!

Reflections:

One pertinent reflection: an enduring gesture will be forever remembered. He placed his thumbs face down, pressed them together and arched his fingers over them and it formed a perfect heart. I was awe-struck. The simplicity of his cleverness mesmerized me.

> I'm smiling now
> my heart is melting at such
> a heartfelt gesture!

His comment back then was, "Hang with me and I can show you a lot of things!" I remembered, I was speechless. What could I say? I said, nothing! :)

elor And The Married Man!

n, a bachelor and a married one. Continuing with
of what happens after eighty concerns two of
these lively friends a bachelor button and a
ve flowers capable of easily lifting anyone's

is the wildflower! The other, an amiable single
a bachelor button flower. These fellows work
troduced them and they are friends. The married
', hence the nickname I gave him. He reminded
tchy song, 'Hey good-lookin,' what cha got
him, as he is a great chef.
nickname is 'Superman!' Why? Because, one
t to 'costume up' for work. He entered Ming
ime, scanned his choices and settled for the
superman tee. He was about to walk out when I hollered, "you
can't go back to work with your regular clothes on."

So he peeled off his shirt and – I gulped and crowed, "Oh my
gosh, you really didn't need a costume, you could just go back to
work looking like that!"

He blushed. He was 'body-perfect!'

One day after work Superman, glad to see me, gave me a hug.
Suddenly a voice boomed behind him, "Hey, leave her alone!" It was
Good-Lookin'!

Flabbergasted, Superman appealed to me, "Tell him we're
friends!" Uh-oh. To ease the conflict, I looked at Superman and asked
him a question about Good-Lookin'.

do you know his nickname?
"No" — "Ho Yerng" I replied,
and he mimicked me

"Perfect," I said, astonished at Superman's diction of the Chinese language. (Ho Yerng means 'good-looking.')

The tension dissipated. Now my question, was this for real?

Real enough!

A few weeks later... Life repeated the same episode in reverse! This time Good-Lookin' was talking to me when Superman shouted, "Leave her alone!"

A startled Good-Lookin' lost for words, grimaced and barked back, "YOU leave me alone!"

Ahhh, was that for real also?

Those are my questions for any role models out there! Help!

After these encounters, each of these 'guys' separately began to call me, 'Beautiful!' I wondered why. I surmised they had been talking about me and the positive result was my new nickname!

Amazing — LIFE's flowers continues to surprise me...

Then my ultimate, enlightening surprise:

I found the answers to my questions after my daily morning of 'quietness' in which I pray 'prayers of thanksgiving' for my life, read my 'daily spirituals' and see everything in 'divine order.'

What came through was 'Unconditional Love.' Not the romantic or familial love, but:

The Love which embraces 'everyone and all things in life — unconditionally.'

Another question was answered unexpectedly while reordering cards for the store, my eyes fell upon a unique flower design. The message inside was:

'To be beautiful, means to be yourself.'
            ~ Thich Nhat Hanh

In The Mirror Who Do I See?

I looked in the mirror this bright morning and beheld my grandma! Eighty-one years later her image became clear. It was me looking like her!

That was a revelation as her image had almost completely faded from my mind. When I was about four years old my grandma came to visit me at the Home. This was her first visit. Upon entering the living room I had no idea why this stern-looking woman dressed in black was staring at me.

The teacher spoke, "Nona this is your grandmother." I looked at her dark black eyes and felt ill at ease. Her piercing eyes bored into me and she seemed to be analyzing every feature of my round face!

Grandma had not seen me since I was three months old, for I had suddenly disappeared from her life! After my father's death, my independent mother tired of her mother-in-law's disposition and of the family's farm life in rural Palo Alto walked out with me and never went back.　The two of us came to live in San Francisco's Chinatown until I was two and went to the orphanage. And now this morning I saw clearly and realized after all these years why my grandma had stared at me so openly. She, as a grandma, was once again seeing herself as a child as l resembled her! Funny indeed, because she was not one of my favorite relatives and now I see her every day!

Grandma was left in China by grandpa for twenty years trying to strike it rich in 'Gold Mountain!' He never did, but he didn't forget her; back he went, crossing the ocean once again to bring grandma to America. Everyone said, "Grandpa was the nice one!"

So each morning I greet the woman in the mirror, "Hi grandma!"

> generations passed
> are we 'mocking' each other?
> I liked what I saw!

Number Eight Is Powerful!

Grandpa left China to strike it rich in the gold mines. He never made it. Instead, he toiled for twenty years growing the best vegetables in rural Mayfield, now Palo Alto. From what I've gathered from relatives, with Grandpa working long hours, he was never around the house, which made Grandma a harried woman in charge of the household.

The closest Grandpa came to any wealth was the day I was born! Born on the eighth day of the month was a cause for jubilation, as the eight number in China represented wealth. It was the most coveted number to be had.

Therefore, Grandpa and Grandma named me Gold and Silver.

I was an 'eight' child, destined for 'the better things in life.' That line came from a learned uncle who read my calligraphy as such! As the soft-spoken, refined teacher at the Home transposed my Grandparents words to mean, the 'better things in life.' Now I wonder, did Grandma have two reasons to glare at me when I was a child? One, because I resembled her as a child? The second reason because of my birthday status? Which did not bring them any material wealth!

Ellen, my oldest half-sister, recalled Grandma and Grandpa chanting: "Yah Gum, Yah Nough," which meant, 'I would have gold and I would have silver.'

In the world of Numerology, if you have an eight in your sign, it represents power and great wealth. I've analyzed people's names and birthdates and find them amazingly accurate, especially the signs of well-known individuals.

I was the 'Numerologist' at my store and enjoyed discovering people's potential in numbers. Later, I was asked to cover two private parties for my Ming Quong customers. Some party-goers were doubtful, but upon analyzing their numbers were astounded at what they represented! Many could see clearly how the numbers in their lives had affected them.

Reflections:

Not one for math, I'm surprised Numerology spoke to me. Joe found my first Numerology book in the 1970's at the Alameda Flea Market. My curious mind absorbed its contents and it has made my life stimulating. I've learned, keeping an open mind is the key to all aspects of life.

universal laws?
Chinese? Numerology?
discover them all...

There are many more 'eight' meanings in this world, as in other cultures.

Sunday Comics

time for a break
Contra Costa Times
reading 'Wee Pals'

I've always enjoyed reading Morrie Turner's comic strip because of his introduction of minority personalities and their achievements.

Morrie, an African-American man was the only syndicated artist cartoonist to take on that venue in 1965. I never knew whose face would come to life in his strip, especially people I knew like Ben Fong Torres of Rolling Stones, William Wong, an investigative journalist, Roberta Wong Murray, a TV reporter, and other familiar icons from the past. Billy Eckstein, a well-known jazz singer, was another favorite.

My mini break at the store in between customers was to skim through the newspaper while I munched on my sandwich. This particular day it was a window changing day for the Christmas season.

This meant less time for relaxing. I quickly zoomed in on his column which featured an Asian-looking woman with glasses and black hair. She looked familiar. Reading on, the young boys and girls were conversing amongst themselves about an author who was an orphan and had written two books and her name was:

'Nona Mock Wyman'

Oh my gosh, I was reading about myself.

"It's me!" I gasped to Jim and his employee Sophie.

Yes, Morrie Turner had surprised me again. The first time he had placed me in his Sunday's 'Soul Corner' was in 2007 as Willie Kee who worked for Channel 2, and Darlene Lee had told him about my book *Chopstick Childhood* which describes my life in a Chinese girls orphanage.

I promptly thanked him and requested the original drawing, which people do as Darlene related to me. Morrie complied and signed it, 'With respect and admiration.'

Now this second appearance was his own doing and this time he included my second book, *Bamboo Women*. I was amazed.

> humbled beyond words
> the year 2013
> harken to a gift

I gulped down my lunch and excitedly trimmed the strip and placed it inside my *Bamboo Women* book which was displayed on the counter. But it didn't look right there.

Where to put it? The Christmas window! Perfect. Placed next to my favorite handmade Christmas card used every year in the window was the auspicious spot. The card made by Vicky Hanson, a young fan of the store, was a tradition. The 1970's card simply stated:

"Happy Birthday Jesus" with a bright star of David.

I surrounded the card and the strip with serene Buddhas as in reverent meditation.

> it felt good
> smiling, I wanted to share
> this with Morrie

Alas, Morrie's address was at home, but my customer, Lisa Wrenn, the feature editor for the Walnut Creek Journal, had seen the strip so she immediately forwarded my 'thank-you email letter' to Morrie.

I was hoping with all my heart that maybe, just maybe, he might be in Walnut Creek shopping for Christmas and surprise me in person!

But, unbeknownst to me, he was gravely ill. Just two weeks later the news reported his passing.

Morrie sadly
departed this world
my tears prayed...

Reflections:

A friend, Dorothy Eng, is a friend with Morrie Turner's sister, so I was able to express my gratitude to the sister for her brother's goodness.

Articles were written following his death. One mentioned that Charles Schultz of the Peanuts comic strip had encouraged Morrie to include minorities in his column as Morrie had originally wanted Charles Shultz to do it!

Then lastly, in a special section of the Sunday comics, a memorable tribute to Morrie Turner naming him:

'The Father of Diversity'

"Wee Pals" featuring Nona by Morrie Turner

"Soul Corner" featuring Nona by Morrie Turner

Follow The Leader

year of the Ox — I'm
right behind the President
following 'The Leader'

I'm right behind the President of the United States, Barack Obama. I followed in his footsteps where he once tread! Really? That was a surprise for me too!

But I'm ahead of my story.

I was actually walking towards the renowned bookstore, 'Book Passage' in Corte Madera, California. Upon entering their courtyard with my driver, Barbara Wagner, my 4 Life-Factor friend, I could see it resembled a trendy resort where specialty coffees and enticing food were served on the inviting patio.

It was the classiest bookstore I'd ever been in.

Classy also because after the hostess for the evening realized we had foregone dinner to get to the reading, she insisted we pick something from the deli menu! Mmm mmm. My eyes chose the creamy-looking macaroni and cheese, baked perfectly golden! Absolutely heavenly. To top it off, we spied my customers from Walnut Creek and joined their table. They were enjoying their desserts.

Once again, our hospitable hostess prodded us to pick a dessert.

We declined, oh so graciously!

After that unexpected gourmet treat, I was ready for the evening. I was there to read and discuss my second book, *Bamboo Women*. In the 'reading room,' I noticed many photos of well-known authors lining the top ridges of the wall. These photos were celebrated authors. Many were PBS television guests who had read at this establishment.

Showcased nicely on a 'pillar' was — The President, Barack Obama.

"Barack Obama had a reading here?" I asked incredulously.

"Yes," the hostess smiled.

So there I was, following the leader!

I had not faithfully kept up with the reading circuit for years because of my own writing and completely missed Obama's appearance at this famed bookstore. So tonight, I would actually walk up to the same stage and use the same podium Obama had used! Exhilarating.

What an auspicious booking, thanks to my publisher, China Books.

It took me back to my childhood days at the Ming Quong orphanage, when we would precariously balance ourselves as we zigzagged crazily around the yard with our arms outstretched and shout at the top of our lungs:

'follow the leader.'

But this time it was for real!

I was fortunate, for that evening our small, intimate group of ten to fifteen people was what any author would desire! They included that special group we shared our meal with from Walnut Creek, who were associated with Kaiser Hospital.

The retired medical doctor, and a retired psychiatrist Mary Olowin, who has become a friend, both wore Ming Quong outfits.

So I joyfully had them stand up and we had a mini 'fashion show,' which included Barbara Wagner.

The women — 'standing tall' — radiated.

Barbara always wore a Ming Quong outfit when she accompanied me to my readings. It was a prerequisite in her mind!

At my readings, if there was anyone in the audience who sported anything from the store, even if it was a tiny piece of jewelry, I would always introduce them. Much more fun that way!

Then adding to my happiness a late comer, Vera Zaskevich, quietly sauntered in hoping not to call attention to her tardiness! She was adorned with a wrist full of jangling bracelets, some of them representing Ming Quong.

At least she was standing! A one-woman show!

Vera is a long-time representative for many gift companies at my store. I've known her for over forty years. This accommodating woman would spend the entire day at the store while Jim and I pondered our selections.

When it was lunchtime, Vera would treat us to whatever we desired! A generous soul.

We'd come back loaded with lunch specials, usually from the Modern China Café. Between savory bites, she filled me with her witty remarks and I couldn't stop laughing. That (she) was my 'dessert!' But I always had our favorite available, coffee candy from Trader Joes.

I dubbed Vera my '#1 Marin editor.' She hails from Marin and she edits and prints out some of my haibun for me, as my poor printer fell and died! What a grand 'rep.' Also, what a way to write a book! I wing it and see everything in 'divine order.'

Now with Vera present, I introduced her. Asked her a pertinent question (can't recall what it was), but she answered in a way no one ever expected, which electrified the room.

The room rocked. Vera was like that. Witty.

Another special woman in the audience was Dinah Scaggs, with her friend Shay. Dinah was the wonderful 'Nanny' for Rhoda Wing's (former Ming Quong alumna) grand-children.

Also present was China Book's representative and a sprinkling of local people.

All these special people made my evening complete.

Meanwhile, that very same evening across the Bay, many fans were transfixed on the Oakland A's baseball playoffs.

While here at Book Passage, I had what I called a 'historical happening' — being here was like batting a 'grand-slam!'

When the evening ended, the hostess handed me a smart looking package, nicely wrapped, entwined with a gossamer bow. Inside, layers upon layers of white tissue. Hidden underneath this cloud, a bundle of ivory-colored note cards. Across the top of the cards, an embossment— 'Nona Mock Wyman.'

I wondered if President Obama and the other speakers received these 'personalized' cards. For me, it was the most satisfying gift received from a book store.

I surmised that all their guests felt similarly 'blessed' like I had been.

Barak Obama
born the 'Year of the Ox'
sign of a 'leader'…

With Arms Wide Open — Los Gatos Welcomes Us Home

Ten thousand flowers strewn along your pathway. That's what it was like coming home for the grandest 'reunion' at the Los Gatos Museum.

Yelda Rivera Laxton, the new curator for the museum, discovered my *Chopstick Childhood* book, about life at the Chinese girl's orphanage and knew this history was meant for a historic exhibit of the Ming Quong Home. With her expertise, and her former Smithsonian background, the exhibit was spectacular.

> streaming banners, photos
> depicting Ming Quong's history
> immortalized

Donaldina Cameron, the founder and rescuer of 'needy girls' and all the former teachers at the 'Home' would have been filled with the spiritual meaning of Ming Quong — 'Radiant Light.'

We Ming Quong women, with their families and friends were filled with pride. And it was extra meaningful to see my customers from the Ming Quong store. I was awestruck at what Yelda had created. Also presented before us that day, a perfect lunch:

> dim sum and dumplings
> along with Chef Rhoda's treat
> beyond delicious...

> standing room only
> as I spoke, thanking all for
> this auspicious time

After reading from *Chopstick Childhood* I paid homage to the Ming Quong Home's first 'caretaker,' Charles Torrey, for donating my book to the museum.

Reflections:

Ever grateful for Yelda and her 'workers and volunteer helpers,' one may catch a rerun of the Ming Quong Home exhibit intertwined with the history of Los Gatos on the televised, 'Eye on the Bay' program.

During that era, it must have been unsettling to many of the retired folks in Los Gatos to see the Chinese girls coming into town. One former MQH alumni said, "Ours was history — hidden under the rug!"

One former classmate of mine thought we were wealthy children bought over from China to protect us from the war! The true history came her way after reading my book, Chopstick Childhood in a Town of Silver Spoons.

Which brings to mind the book-reading I gave for the Los Gatos Presbyterian Church. That day their lunch table decoration was a floral display with bamboo surrounded by sterling silver spoons with a pair of chopstick laid across each spoon. It was something to behold. Like the Bible verse we learned and heard at church,

"My cup runneth over..." I clearly felt the impact.

We ended by singing, 'In Christ there is no East or West...'

Walnut Creek's Gone Green

forty-seven years
no more plastic bags
paper only

Yes, in the beginning all we used were paper bags and I'd personalized them with the Chinese Ming Quong symbol. I loved it! Now Walnut Creek's new law as of September 18, 2014, all stores will use paper bags so that the environment and landfills would be less hazardous for all living things.

I explained to a customer that now ten cents a bag would be charged if they needed one. She was OK with that so I automatically filled her bag with her purchases and handed it to her. Thanking me, she left. Then a second later, I realized I had used a regular plastic bag, which was still at my fingertips!

After forty-seven years in business, things come automatically. So engrossed in our 'fun chatting' we both never noticed. A few days later two dark-skinned fellows shopped for some artifacts and once again, I repeated that Walnut Creek had gone 'green' and so had our store, then I added, "but I'm really 'yellow.'"

The buyer's response,

"And I'm really black, but I'm also yellow!"

all around, laughter
keep it light, keep it fun
use your hands, they're free

Reflections:

A regret: the three of us had so much fun laughing I never asked him — what his 'yellow' meant!

Haiku
Senryu
Tanka
Part Two

An Unusual Happening At The Store

bright morning
she makes a purchase
with a fake credit card
~ jerry ball
was present at the store...

now they've caught the thief
the postman wants to know
if she was pretty
~ jerry ball

up in the air blonde
black credit card purchase
hand-cuffed at City Hall...
~ Jim Wyman

after school shopping
the girl wants to buy a mood ring
for one of her toes!
~ nona

summer afternoon
the shopkeeper sees a dress
she sold yesterday
~ jerry ball
for nona

Sheryl, my niece has
three sons, Brandon the oldest
and twin boys
their names — Aidon
and Christopher

Aidon looks like me
Big Eyes and all
says my sister

Brandon looks like my
sister – expression and all
says their Aunt 'No'

Christopher looks like
both 'sisters' with his
smile...

> ~ Aunt 'No'
> *tanka and haiku for Sheryl,*
> *her sons and my sister, Lonnie*

Zoe is sixteen
candidly outspoken
just like a Mock!

> ~ nona
> *cousin to the three boys above...*

advice from the
teacher will come
when you are ready

> ~ nona

summer at the store
telling her the truth, she said,
"you made my day..."

    ~ nona
       for Marie C Szantai, dubbed the #1
       Feng Shui guru for Contra Costa
       County by Diablo Magazine

a little sharp
sometimes flat
snoring orchestra

    ~ Mack — 4th grader

birders listening
mockingbirds imitating
songbirds

    ~ Brian Murphy & nona

fragrant smells of time
nature abounds in bird song
nesting in jasmine

    ~ Deb Van Laak

ding, ding, bus driver
having fun, proclaiming our
store to her riders

    ~ nona
       the trolley bus driver is a MQ
       customer, who drove by at the exact
       time this 'new' book arrived!

grand old library
we said our 'good-byes' with 'love
messages on walls...
~ nona

4/20/2005 1st row: Sally, Bob Schroder (former Mayor) Nona Wyman
2nd row: Brad Rovenpera, historian--Cindy Britten, head librarian

Walnut Creek Library – "Uncovered Stories" Panel Discussion

Panelist Sally subbed for Ruth Bancroft who was not feeling well.

Ruth Bancroft's age
one hundred and seven in
two thousand fifteen

History revealed
on Walnut Creek's past
by ancient seniors!

way before our time
Walnut Creek's first murder
in Target's parking lot

in the audience
an original customer
from Ming Quong

for Judi Sullivan
a Benicia artist whose soul shines
through...

Reflections:

The 'Ruth Bancroft gardens' in Walnut Creek are famous for her succulents. People from all over attend annual tours to purchase prized plants.

And — the next generation...

behind the counter
Erica selling silver
jewelry at Ming Quong

~ Erica
granddaughter to Ruth Bancroft
who now models and appears in TV
commercials

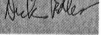

Dick Bolles

pencil sketching
authors at book readings
no eraser!
~ nona

Amy Tan

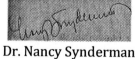

Dr. Nancy Synderman

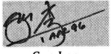

Gus Lee

Lisa See

left-handed artist
attempts to draw and listen
at the same time

~ nona

Gail Tsukiyama

Peter Coyote

Sketched at Jackie's well-liked 'Bonanza Books' store in Walnut Creek. Her store was the 'light' at the other end of the Caldecott tunnel. Also named one of the "7 Wonders of the East Bay."

'Melting Pot' restaurant
served burgers named after 'stores'
'Ming Quong' — "teriyaki..."
'Thrift Store' — "plain"
I'm hungry — what's for lunch?
> ~ nona
> *for Tim and Marguerite's popular fondue haunt.*
> *The former premise was the popular Nut Bowl*
> *delicatessen and is now the Ojai restaurant.*

challenging myself
to sell more Chinese candy
for a gourmet treat
> ~ nona
> *for Aromatica's Karene Biderman's 'gourmet*
> *treats'. This location now features Walnut*
> *Creek's famous Italian restaurant, 'Prima.'*

daughter recalls
her favorite haiku
by her father
> ~ nona
> *for K. Ball – Jerry Ball's daughter*

winter morning
I try to remember the dream
I began as a child
> ~ jerry ball
> *K's favorite haiku*

like the earth
haiku is understated
it doesn't explain
> ~ nona
> *from a 'workshop lesson' by Jerry*
> *Ball*

mountain to mountain
hundreds of prayer flags soaring
like migrating birds
> ~ nona

winter day
being a good listener
drains my energy
> ~ Delia White
> *'for Nona'*

thank you for being
because you are just enough
of God's creation
> ~ Zoe Maclean

November chill
the manzanita meet me
with blooms
> ~ Anastasia Hobbet
> *A helpful friend, author and founder*
> *of 'Diablo Writers Workshop'*

dainty raindrops dance
ringlets cheer the swollen pond
wrinkling it in smiles
> ~ Christine Horner
> *haiku winner and author*

on the crowded train
a stranger talks to himself
we pretend not to hear
> ~ Cristiana Moline

my life is written
one wise fortune at a time
in Chinese cookies

~ LaDonna Fehlberg
author, photographer & award-winning poet at the Alameda County Fair 2016

you thought you were bad
but you were hot
you sounded good!

~ Dave Rogers for 'Nona'
former neighbor, Dave recorded my 1st book-reading at Mills College.

I listened and was
amazed — my voice came through
unlike my 'phone voice...'

~ nona
for Dave — musician and a traveler. He said, "a haiku is always read twice at poetry readings in Japan."

Dave Roger's three 'in the moment' haiku composed at the store!

the kids use short tweets
to communicate today
oh for the old days

where we use to live
lizards under every rock
that is where we played

now I'm so refreshed
feel like I just did yoga
just like time at Mills

see what haiku
can do for you
everyone — try it!
    ~ nona

historic — rooster
crowing for Chinese New Year's
"I'm a stamp!"
    ~ nona
        rooster stamp in 2005 – followed by
        the 12 Zodiac animals

high-tech computer
even has windows, what for?
fresh air and a view?
    ~ nona
        appeared in Angela Hill's column—
        2015 Bay Area newspapers

suckling baby
observes his new world
burps with pleasure
    ~ nona
        for Brenda Wong Aoki and son, KK
        (daughter of Bessie Wong, a MQH
        girl)

sometimes I forget
I'm Chinese, does that really
matter – I'm me!
    ~ nona

"what took you so long?"
"I was outside working
on my tan."
> ~ nona
> *for Dwayne, our tall-dark-and-*
> *handsome, African-American mail-*
> *carrier*

upon hearing that
he might be in my book: "good, it
will be a best-seller!"
> ~ nona
> *for Dwayne*

breezing in — the
mailman greets me
"Hi, Winona Ryder!"
> ~ nona
> *for Rod, our former 'humorous' mail*
> *carrier*

wrinkles are good
says the sports doctor
how about my face?
> ~ nona

simple, just follow
doctor's order – "exercise"
wrinkles gone!
> *~ nona*
> *both haiku for Dr. Al, (revered by all)*
> *1st haiku shared with appropriate*
> *patients — 2nd haiku about the*
> *latest 2016 survey shows; when you*
> *exercise, you'll feel better & you'll*
> *look younger! :)*

spring green
crisp as a Fuji apple
yikes, a worm!
~ nona

a dog sits down
he starts to eat
then he falls asleep
~ Adam — 4th grade

frog hopping
throat inflates
sweet sounds
~ Mack — 4th grade

his master arrives
the puppy becomes a mass
of wiggly ways
~ jerry ball

on the classroom wall
paintings of cherry blossoms
all masterpieces
~ nona
in Sandy Ball's 5th grade class

cherry blossom branch
blowing in the wind
snap -- it broke...
~ 5th grade student
*Note - the lesson was the art of
'blowing paint through a straw.'*

Chinese New Year's Parade In San Francisco, Ca. (2010)

Martha Mew, former Ming Quong alumna & granddaughter Kristina

a passing float with
Kristina from Lafayette
'First Princess'

Chinese Princess
spokesman for her culture
barely speaks Chinese

~ nona
*for Kristina — she did take a crash
course in Chinese and did well.
Beautiful both inside and out – her 2nd
honorary title — 'Miss Chamber of
Commerce, USA'.*

Nona, the author
her life in a special book
brings tears to my eyes
    ~ Lani Owyoung
        daughter of Martha Mew & mother
        to Kristina

express as haiku
helps me to write down my thoughts
feelings flow freely
    ~ Lani Owyoung

the eyes see the image
but the heart
sees the real person
    ~ Kelley Kwong
        grand-daughter of Beverly Chew
        (MQ gal)

look-a-like beauties
observed each other's image
and beheld themselves!
    ~ nona
        for Brenda and Eta

Note:

    Brenda is the daughter of MQ alumna, Bessie Wong Aoki.

    Eta is the daughter of MQ alumna, Nona Mock Wyman! An 'honor'
bestowed me by Eta's mother.

not my cup of tea
prefer to slice, dice and chop
pass the rice, please!
> ~ Chef Rhoda Wing
> *MQH gal – not into writing haiku!*

savor the season
dance into strawberry dreams
plunge into shortcakes
> ~ nona
> *after shopping at Trader Joe's*

green tea brûlée
soft cloud floating
on my tongue
> ~ Carol, Terry, Nona
> *Friends, after lunch at SaSa*

Maure Quilter
initials 'MQ' has lunch
with 'MQ' alumna
> ~ nona
> *for Maure, who radiates the*
> *meaning of "MQ's" 'Radiant Light'*

Be My Voice!

near the old oak tree
a local book store welcomes
it's newest author

rainforest orchids
magenta in color
grace the book display

on the wicker couch
the cat snuggles between us
listening...

two fellow writers
critique each other's books
now – published authors

similar in taste
both authors sipping
ginger tea...

cat darts off
as line forms for author's
book signing

Tom, the cordial host
serves wine and cheese
to the large crowd

~ nona

For Cinda Mackinnon, whose 'voice went in and out' leaving her
almost 'speechless!' Her book, 'A Place in the World.' It was the only
book I allowed myself to read during the writing of my Bamboo
Women book! Cinda and I were in the Diablo's Writers Group. 'Our'
reading was at the Orinda Book store.

You are here
the door always open
the smile welcomes
~ Michael H. Day
for Nona

Michael is the guy I saw and palled around with 25 years ago, along with his son, Christopher, at the grand opening for the Regional Center for the Arts. We were on the outside, looking in! And then today almost 25 years later I was talking about him and his haiku when he walks in, only moments before I was ready to send this page off to my publisher! This episode happens frequently! We're on the same wavelength!

So now I was able to add his above haiku to *the book*!

And my haiku for Michael is:

divine happening
his presence — his haiku — plus
a new haiku book!
~ nona
for Michael H. Day (his 2nd surprise
for me — a beautiful haiku book)

conceived in desire
roots reaching up to heaven
we return to the stars
~ Michael H. Day

Reflections:

The above Center, all sparkling and glamorous, now known as the Lesher Center for the Arts, once housed the monstrous building called 'The Nut House' where walnuts once ruled!

receiving a hug
with her tiny arms
warms my whole being
> ~ nona and jerry ball

summer afternoon
silhouettes of children
playing in the shadow
> ~ nona and jerry ball

meditating
eyes closed — group listened to my
words — calmness happened!
> ~ nona
> *lead a meditation for a 'Woman to*
> *Woman' retreat at Stanford*
> *University (E. Rathbun/host –*
> *renown thinker and activist)*

Ming Quong store was once
the 'lobby' of the 'Walnut
Creek Hotel'
upstairs, small guest rooms
now small offices
> ~ nona

'a first' — Eichler homes
welcoming all races to
'small town' Walnut Creek
> ~ nona
> *former owner of an Eichler.*
> *Joseph Eichler, a leader whose*
> *homes throughout California are*
> *famous and revered for its modern*
> *architecture of the 1940's*

a straw-bale house
not in never-never land
but in Walnut Creek

~ nona

for Bob Joe's Ecohouse (2003); first
2-story steel house in the world!

in all the seasons
children standing tall
projecting Oneness

~ nona

Benny Bufano's statue at Civic Park,
Walnut Creek

sunrise, sunset
lunar eclipse, super moon
all in one day

~ nona

same day — 'Asian
Moon Festival' cosmos
mingling with the stars

~ nona

spectacular 'sky show' 9/27/2015

coming home — I know
it's Wednesday — driveway spotless
fallen leaves — poof — gone!
our neighbor's gardener
included us — I'm thankful...

~ nona

for our neighbors, Wayne & Carol

handicapped parking
in San Francisco — watch out
yellow zones — no? — yes!

~ nona

sounds of a new friend
walking beside me
my cane

~ nona

eighty years plus, 'twin
sisters' in many ways
sporting their 'twin canes'

~ nona
for Jennie, my 'smiling twin' from the
MQH

Tuesday night poets
without Jerry – our mentor
our hearts are heavy
yet his presence envelopes us
a Oneness is felt...

~ nona
for Jerry Ball
whose new Parkinson medication
made him miss a session for the 1st
time in 7 years!

Death haiku were written by the haiku masters of the past.

beyond words
beautiful
aching...
~ nona

this song of yours, Finch...
will I hear it again
in the next world?
~ jerry ball

weeping for kindness
at the passing of a friend
a summer's end
~ jerry ball

the clothing salesman
wrapped in sorrow
dying of AIDS
at the end — the final touch
giant ribbon — red roses
~ nona
*'tanka' for Harry Sallada, 1st
clothing 'rep.'*

love tattoos are 'stars'
each arm completely covered
names a good friend
~ nona
*for Craig Williams, a 'rep.' for Harry,
Harry's star is on his arm...*

on hospital bed
hands clasped together
the atheist prays

> ~ nona
> *for Uncle Henry, the elitist*
> *intellectual*

late afternoon
the mantis still praying
in the sage

> ~ Susan Antolin
> *author, award-winning poet, and*
> *secretary for the Haiku Society of*
> *America*

though the flowers of fall
perish in winters fierce cold
we will not forget

> ~ Kelley Kwong
> *for her grandmother's memorial;*
> *Beverly Chew, my lifelong friend,*
> *beginning at MQH.*

the wisdom and truth
deep within his winter soul
waiting for release

> ~ nona
> *for Joe, belated husband*

writing a haibun
for a friend's passing
lifts the heart

> ~ nona
> *for Mary Spivey*

moonlight fire
glowing ember red
forest crying

~ nona
  California's horrendous fires

each rose, each flower
is a calling card of
life beyond...

~ nona

orbiting 'China-
Town in the Sky' – friends, moon and
stars rejoicing...

~ nona
  *for Luella Wong Mak, a MQ alumna's
  2016 memorial @ Chabot
  Observatory located at:
  10000 Skyline Blvd in Oakland, Ca.!*

eyes bright with love
toddler running to hug
grandpa and grandma

~ nona
  *for Lexis's son; toddler's
  grandparents are Walt & Maribel
  Wong Ng (MQ gal, sister to Luella.)*

Gratefulness

echoes of joy
etched between the pages
of memories

I turn and pause
in gratitude
and thankfulness

walking in my
ancestors' footsteps – I
gather more flowers

Haibun

Part Three

Unbelievable

I can't believe I'm writing this 2nd edition before the 1st edition has had a chance to fully bloom!

But, because this might be the last book I write, I've needed to include a meaningful happening which was left out!

This concerned Colleen, a customer and her desire.

> always a dream to
> work at Ming Quong – one Spring day
> her dream came true

And from there, she became what I call a 'fierce spirit;' speaking her mind for the store she loved.

When our lease was in jeopardy, she appeared on Facebook and rallied 200 supporters!

Some signed petitions while others were even ready to demonstrate in front of our store!

As you know – our lease was renewed!

Thank you Colleen and all our loyal supporters.

Reflections:

On a different vein: I shy away from 'demos.' But once I actually instigated one!

> ringing City Hall
> "demo permit needed"
> granted – no problem

Absolutely simple! That is, after the authorities realized it was to be a 'cooking demo' by Chef Rhoda Wing. :)

Life Continues On...

as in life
as in writing
corrections needed

Nothing like reading a book by 'yours truly' that has no errors. On this second edition I'm attempting to do the impossible! Given this chance for corrections – I'm including the entire book!

Here's a scholarly observation – when the word impossible is divided – it becomes 'I'm – possible!' So maybe there's a possibility! :) Oops – except I just added a smile face – so right away that's a literary wrong!

But continuing on, I once heard a musician offering advice to a singer, "Be true to yourself and stand out." I would say that statement pertains to my 'smile faces' as seen in my Ming Quong newsletters. Those cute faces are such a part of me that my 'left hand' automatically types it out and I feel complete! :) So because this may be my last book, I'll just keep on smiling and 'be true to myself.' :)

In fact, at the latest Book-of-the-Month-Club, a woman's comment was, "You're always smiling!"

Now after corrections, additions and 'mislaid material' added, I've added more haibun/chapters. Which is like writing my 4th book!

Oh, the life of a writer! :)

Continuing on...

One haibun is out of the norm, when I talked with my mouth full and what came out of me! Another one – when I was like a 'weed' in a room of plenty! The other was a fun discovery within this book and my soul sang!

And much more as life continues on...

A New Discovery

A little gem of a 'coloring book' manifested itself right before my eyes and...

when I looked again, I saw clearly that it was in this book – my new book!

'Ten Thousand Flowers!'

And now, I ask you – did you see it?
Yes or no, here's two tanka and a haiku explaining it all...

take a second look
each flower drawing has grown
bursting it's seeds
its pollen into a field
of unparalleled beauty

a well-planned drawing
perfect for coloring...
the 'new-found method' for
meditation – plus...
relaxing the whole body

so go for it
color all six pages
enjoy – have fun!

The 'coloring pages – of the cosmo flowers' by Ana Vee starts on the Title page then follows pages – 18, 54, 68, 144 and 171.

Ana attended the California College of the Arts and when she graduated (2016) the class donned 'berets,' a tradition, which is so befitting! Talented Ana is a Ming Quong part-time employee, who recently received her '1st art assignment.'

A Hana (Flower) Experience

What could be more appropriate – my first book reading for 'Ten Thousand Flowers' to be held at a restaurant named – 'Hana...' – which means a flower.

It was the Year of the Monkey and I was the guest speaker for the Association for Chinese Cooking Teachers (ACCT). A perfect way to celebrate Chinese New Year especially because I enjoy eating! That day I discovered seaweed salad and I was in sushi heaven!

> star-rated restaurant
> 'Hana Zen' smorgasbord
> fit for connoisseurs

Located at the far-end of Pier 39 with an unobstructed view of the newly lit Bay Bridge, and the crashing waves, with diving seagulls and luxury-looking ferry boats. I was mesmerized.

The beginning of a wonderful evening. But, alas, it wasn't!

In fact, in my 'book-reading' experience, I would call this one a – 'weed!'

A weed with plenty of thorns! For instance, one was an abrupt change – my forty minute talk was cut to ten minutes – and when I joked about it to the audience no one heard me. In fact the listeners called, out "Mic, mic – we can't hear you!"

Oh my gosh! My awkward hand-held mike didn't work for me...

Nevertheless, I bent over to deliver my talk – but the lighting was much too dim for my notes! And I had nowhere to move for better lighting – so decided to just wing it – but then – the space for my notes was a narrow ledge, and one of my papers fluttered to the floor!

It was a truly awkward situation as the restaurant was split, an upper and lower level, and I was on the top level.

By that time I was beyond frustration, I spoke only five minutes of my allotted time and utterly didn't say anything truly pertinent!

I felt emotionally drained and felt I'd let my audience down!

But my dilemma didn't end there!

During the long line for the buffet, a smiling woman acknowledged me. She had impressed me earlier with her graciousness, but in particular I noticed how smartly dressed she was with her striking red turban and her free-swinging black dress. I remarked on her outfit. She replied simply – that she had cancer!

> at a loss for words
> I nodded in silence
> signing her three books

She had earlier purchased a 'set' of my books – the first person ever to buy all three – as Lani Owyoung, my 'tuned-in' friend had graciously walked from table to table (because of my knee problem) telling people the story of my life.

Later, in line for the buffet, this woman acknowledged me and paused at my table. She leaned on my shoulder as I waited for her to speak, but nothing came forth. As she leaned closer she got heavier and my face nearly touched my dinner plate.

Perplexed, I turned and glimpsed her closed eyes.

Oh my gosh, she had passed out!

"HELP," I cried out to Dana, Lani's husband, as he quickly grabbed a chair.

Suddenly red liquid spilled from her mouth, followed by vomit.

> paramedics called
> chemo–daiquiri – not a
> good mix...

Reflections:

The poor woman. That evening she spent two hours at the hospital.

The days that followed no one at ACCT answered our inquiries about her welfare. But a week later, with Lani's perseverance she was able to contact the woman by phone. She found her at home reading my Chopstick Childhood book!

> Lani was her 'light'
> the 'L' in Lani's name
> represents – 'LOVE'

I am ever grateful for Dana and Lani. They were my 'flowers,' my supportive light.

'Hana,' a perfect reminder that in the midst of chaos, one can find serenity and beauty.

As for the woman — her graciousness is:

> etched in my mind
> a kind and gentle soul
> forever remembered

Interesting related facts:

> the Oneness of Zen
> two small towns in Maui
> 'Haiku' and 'Hana'

More facts:

About two months later the ACCT president, Doris came to the store and related, "The people enjoyed you!"

"Really?" I exclaimed. "Yes, because the subject was different!"

Then she took a picture of me!

Hmm, the 'Year of the Monkey' promises to be full of unexpected surprises and happenings! :)

But!!!! — I plan to do something different!

I was invited to be a Guest Speaker at the Lafayette Library in November 2016 for the Diablo Valley Chinese Cultural Association. Their theme for the luncheon is, 'Hawaii,' with singers and hula dancers.

So, I thought of my 'new' Hawaiian relatives – as described in this book! (See page 20.)

What a perfect tie-in as this group knows nothing about my heritage!

Should be a different happening as I was once a former DVCCA member!

WOW!

Driving up to a charming home, I was greeted by an unexpected notice.

> the warning sign
> 'BEWARE OF CHIHUAHUA'
> I laughed out loud

How cute was that? I was at my doctor's home for a 'book-of-the-month' club which featured all three of my books.

Absolutely no ferocious dog in sight, but what was before me was a 'wow' scene!

A roomful of chatting, amiable women sipping wine over-looking an azure pool, surrounded by a luscious garden filled with precious flowers, ancient oaks and beyond all this beauty ~ a lake!

Unbelievable, a serene scenario hidden in the suburbs of Walnut Creek.

Treasures inside were esoteric. I was entranced.

The perfect hostess, the wonderful women and the Chinese dinner which embraced my heritage.

While enjoying our dessert, a woman asked, "What does Ming Quong mean?"

I replied with a mouthful, "It means Radiant Light."

"What?" she asked, "Crazy at night?"

> uh-oh I forgot
> 'don't talk with your mouth full' — drilled
> into me at the 'Home'

I'm sure our rousing laughter was heard across the quiet lake! And so amidst all this we composed a senryu/haiku:

Radiant Light
crazy at night
mouthful of cake
~ Cynthia Shambaugh

Fun – fun – fun – and more fun – the little Chihuahua, named Bruiser was let out of a back room when the doctor came home and little Bruiser wiggled happily with love and pure joy enjoying all the crumbs! :)

Reflections:

That evening there were exactly 10 women present.

How auspicious was that?

Each woman representing 10,000 flowers!

Then when the gracious doctor drove me home he said, "They are all your new friends..."

I was speechless. What a caring man!

Beautiful, lovely, gorgeous flowers, which of course includes the doctor and little Bruiser.

And when I asked the name of this 25-year-old group, they replied 'WOW,' which means, 'Women for Words.'

How good is that? :)

Jim was curious why I chose the figure – '10,000' for the book title.

it felt right and the
'10,000' appeared often
it was destined to be!

The Dragon Lady

many years ago
a 'dragon lady' was I
as dubbed by Carol

to a customer
I resembled the 'dragon
lady' – Anna Mae Wong

The first haiku concerning Carol, is the local artist Carol Lutz.
That she called me a 'Dragon Lady' was more or less a
compliment! I think! :) Dragon ladies were known as being in charge
and fierce!

once a clothing 'rep'
thought we were a 'mother
daughter' team!

We laughed and joked about it; because we were worlds apart in
looks and were completely different individuals with varying
viewpoints!
We attended gift shows and a few apparel shows as she worked
for Lissa, who owned the Main Source store on N. Main Street, where
the Brass Bear, a deli, now stands.
Together we shopped, till we dropped. That is – Lissa and Carol
did.
After MS closed, Carol and I continued attending the shows for
years, so we came to know each other better.
Jumping to the present, I now call myself a 'drag-gin lady'
because of my knee, trailing behind her at shows.
Carol is amazing. She's an 'advent' walker.

Then when I turned a mere 58! :) – Carol surprised me with this hand-painted card.

Inside the card was her message: "Happy Dragon Day, Much love, Carol." With a footnote: "Happy Dragon Lady!"

Reflections:

Carol's clever card is at my home gallery, adjacent to a framed black & white portrait of Anna Mae Wong, drawn by Carol's well-known father, Pierre J. Gee; an artist and fashion designer.

It's also next to Anna Mae Wong's one-of-a-kind bracelet with speckles of inlaid abalone shells on a thick black bangle. It's stunning.

Anna gave this bracelet to Carol's mother and she passed it on to me. Too big to wear comfortably, it enhances the area with memories.

And here's a fun fact—once upon a time—the famous actress baby-sat Carol! :)

Is that cute or what?

Anna Mae Wong was Hollywood's 1st notable Chinese-American actress. (1901-1967)

AND NOW –in December of 2016, Carol will celebrate her big one, so:

> happy 90th
> birthday – much love from your
> 'drag-gin lady!'

More Reflections:

For more on Carol, read the haibun, 'Cock-a-doodle-do,' and view the haiga with her Asilomar painting. She is an award-winning artist and has been a judge for the Alameda County Fair.

On The Air!

I was on the air, an educational station in the Los Angeles area. This happened in the first part of the Monkey year, and aired in March. The program was for the – 'Archetypal Mosaic' – on Art, Book, Orphans and Lessons Learned.

on the radio
KPFK – interviewed by
Mikhail Tank

'fifty-two' minutes
answering with 'ums' and pauses!
hope my voice comes through!

I was nervous, yet exhilarated at the same time. My voice was strained as I was on my reclining chair!

It was strange to be talking at home with no one around, only me and a phone and Mikhail's voice! And so I relaxed, yet I had this feeling I shouldn't be relaxing like this, letting myself go as no one was around. But it was my day off and my feet elevated felt good!

After the interview I was exhausted! Like I'd done a day's work!

Later, listening to the interview, I learned a new lesson, sit up straight and let your voice come through!

The responses from some of my listeners were:

"What a beautiful, inspiring interview."

"Thank-you so much for sharing."

"Terrific, I heard it all."

"...exactly what I needed to hear..."

"You truly are a guiding light."
"And down Mikhail's way"
"very deep"
"very spiritual"

I felt relief; I was touched.

My gratitude to Mikhail Tank, the talented interviewer for this experience and for his insightful questions. Mikhail has been a Ming Quong customer since he was a young teen with a uniqueness about him.

KPFK is the sister station to local Berkeley station KPFA.

Internet Locations Nona is Online

The entire audio of the interview is available for download and listening from the website *SoundCloud:*

https://soundcloud.com/user-472824257/nona-kpfk-radio-interviewmp3

There is also a YouTube video interview with Nona; narrated with photos of Nona and other girls from the Ming Quong home. That video is located:

https://www.youtube.com/watch?v=GleFs6O7stA

Enthralling Moments

International
Women's Day – 'Bamboo Women'
picked by Benicia
for their – 'book-of-the-month' club
the 'light' continues

honored indeed
Ming Quong women – customers
sent accolades

*for Linda Lewis, my deepest
appreciation for choosing 'Bamboo
Women.'*

And now one last 'enthralling' moment.

Definitely an unexpected and happiest sign posted on 6/8/2016 by Monica Daigle-Kleisath, an original Ming Quong customer, meaning from the beginning!

Then another heart-warming moment, an article appeared in the Walnut Creek Journal about her signs, so it found a spot in the front window. And there's more, on Sunday it was in all the Bay Area News Group papers! Exciting.

> blossoming hearts
> on Homestead in Walnut Creek
> neighbors blessed

Article by Deborah Burstyn, another Ming Quong customer. I'm smiling... (Note: the Contra Costa Times is now called the East Bay Times.)

Reflections:

Memories of International Women's Day surfaced after the memorial celebration for a MQ alumna, Luella. As a graduate of Mills College, Tommiette Rey of Mills had Luella & I as speakers. Luella had truly come home, for as a child she lived at the 1st MQH which was on the grounds of the college.

Another remembrance – the Women's Studies program at St. Mary's College, under Maureen Little, invited me to speak for International Women Day.

Speaking of 'studies' – my Chopstick Childhood book was required reading at San Mateo College for Asian Studies, by Professor Joe Fong. Bamboo Women, published by China Books, was listed under Asian American Studies.

Looking back: my books educated me!

I now realize the significance of — 'womanhood!'

What Happens Next?

Many years ago, I met this petite woman named Kammy Rose at my very first book-reading for Chopstick Childhood.

We became friends and to this day, I look forward to her emails on esoteric, worldly subjects which are always mind-boggling.

Now to the present – after Kammy read Ten Thousand Flowers she sent me a card with enthralling accolades. And then to my surprise she added her 'first ever haiku' (her words) and made this comment, "How could I resist?"

> enthralling moments
> captured experiences
> now embraced forever
> ~ Kammy Rose

Absolutely beautiful. Kammy had entered the 'Land of Haiku.' And I discovered a new word, 'enthralling.' Each discovery of a good-sounding word is exciting for me. As I used in the previous haibun!

Reflections:

To read more about Kammy, please re-read the haibun in this book, titled, "Uh-Oh!" And be amazed what she did for 'history' many years ago!

So now what happens next? One thing for sure – Kammy has written more haiku! :)

And as you readers know what happened to me when I wrote numerous haiku about living at the Ming Quong Home/Orphanage – it turned into my first book, Chopstick Childhood, followed by Bamboo Women and now, Ten Thousand Flowers!

So, should you feel a stirring within you, grab a pen, jot it down – capture your thoughts, or do what your heart dictates: sing, dance, compose. Life may surprise you.

So come in – share your stories and adventures, or email me ~ nona-mq@webtv.net – you know I'll be smiling. :)

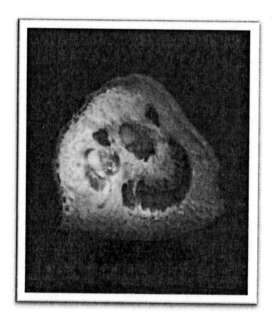

Speaking of smiling, look at this enduring smile, unusual as it comes from an orange peel! Yes, the top of an orange cut the 'Chinese' way! This unique way requires only six slits for the skin to peel away! After years of cutting an orange this way, the above smile appeared!

At that time, I was writing this book about smiles, and my friend Virginia Hallberg, who possessed a gentle spirit, was dying. One day she asked her daughter for an orange and;

this 'significant
smile' from beyond amazed
me — as memories
surrounded me, filling the
moment with joy...

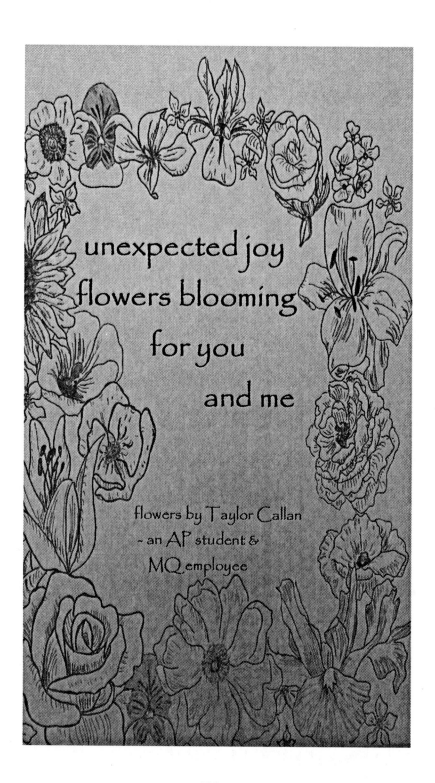

unexpected joy
flowers blooming
for you
and me

flowers by Taylor Callan
~ an AP student &
MQ employee

Photos & Drawings